Timothy McDermott is a retired professor of computer science. He is the editor and translator of *Thomas Aquinas's Summa Theologiae: A Concise Translation*, and of Aquinas's *Selected Philosophical Writings* in the *World's Classics* series.

HOW TO READ

Available now

Forthcoming

HOW TO READ

AQUINAS

TIMOTHY McDERMOTT

Granta Books
London

Granta Publications, 2/3 Hanover Yard, Noel Road, London N1 8BE

First published in Great Britain by Granta Books 2007

A CIP catalogue record for this book is
available from the British Library.

1 3 5 7 9 10 8 6 4 2

ISBN 978–1–86207–914–4

Typeset by M Rules

Printed and bound in Great Britain by
Bookmarque Limited, Croydon, Surrey

CONTENTS

SERIES EDITOR'S FOREWORD

How am I to read *How to Read*?

This series is based on a very simple, but novel idea. Most beginners' guides to great thinkers and writers offer either potted biography or condensed summaries of their major works, or perhaps even both. *How to Read*, by contrast, brings the reader face-to-face with the writing itself in the company of an expert guide. Its starting point is that in order to get close to what a writer is all about, you have to get close to the words they actually use and be shown how to read those words.

Every book in the series is in a way a masterclass in reading. Each author has selected ten or so short extracts from a writer's work and looks at them in detail as a way of revealing their central ideas and thereby opening doors onto a whole world of thought. Sometimes these extracts are arranged chronologically to give a sense of a thinker's development over time, sometimes not. The books are not merely compilations of a thinker's most famous passages, their 'greatest hits', but rather they offer a series of clues or keys that will enable readers to go on and make discoveries of their own. In addition to the texts and readings, each book provides a short biographical chronology and suggestions for further reading, internet resources, and so on. The books in the *How to Read* series don't claim to tell you all you need to know about Freud, Nietzsche and Darwin, or indeed Shakespeare and the Marquis de Sade, but they do offer the best starting point for further exploration.

Unlike the available second-hand versions of the minds that have shaped our intellectual, cultural, religious, political and scientific landscape, *How to Read* offers a refreshing set of first-hand encounters with those minds. Our hope is that these books will, by turn, instruct, intrigue, embolden, encourage and delight.

Simon Critchley
New School for Social Research, New York

ACKNOWLEDGEMENTS

I want to express particular gratitude to my editor, Bella Shand, for her work on this book. I offer the book, by way of apologia, to F. R. J. Crawford, with love.

INTRODUCTION

Thomas Aquinas (1225–74) was the greatest philosopher and theologian of the medieval Christian west. He is divided from us by 800 years of immense social and economic change, which have seen radical reappraisals of the status of religion and science. Yet his theological and philosophical insights remain sharply relevant today, even to the most secularly minded of us. He lived in an age that asked questions about everything all the time: its thinkers were as bold and innovative as its cathedral builders, and Aquinas was the most robust and inventive questioner among them.

Aquinas took as his model the Greek philosopher Aristotle (384–22 BCE), who wrote that 'we all tend to question the views of our opponents rather than the matter in hand, and even when interrogating ourselves push inquiry only to the point where we can no longer offer opposition. But the good inquirer raises the objections demanded by the subject, familiar with all its facets.' Aquinas was a good inquirer, asking questions for their answers' sake in order to make sense of the world – questions on the natural world and living things, on how we sense and understand, on happiness and how to live a human life well, on the structures of human society, on whether there is a God and what religion is about, and on the claims of Christianity

The Middle Ages is traditionally viewed as a period of dark

unreason, sandwiched between the classical civilizations of Greece and Rome and the dawn of modern scientific enlightenment, but it was in fact one of the great periods of intellectual awakening in western Europe. Aquinas, youngest son of an Italian count, was educated first in the Benedictine monastery of Monte Cassino and then in the recently founded secular university of Naples. Here he discovered Aristotle's scientific and philosophical works, which were being translated into Latin for the first time from Greek texts and Arabic translations preserved by Islam. From Aristotle Aquinas learnt that early Greek science had pictured the world as simply material atoms in continual enforced motion, until Aristotle's immediate predecessors, Socrates (470–399 BCE) and Plato (428–348 BCE), had started to ask about the human inclination to pursue truth and virtue. Plato thought such unchanging 'ideas' or 'forms' belonged to an eternal spiritual world only dimly reflected in the bodily world, and accessible only to the immortal human soul: a soul come from the spiritual world to sojourn briefly in the world of matter and at death return to eternity. His student Aristotle, a doctor's son and a biologist, set out to reintegrate these two worlds of matter and forms into the single natural world to which human beings belonged, body and soul. Greek civilization gave way to the Roman empire, which in its later years embraced a Christianity that found Plato's view of soul more attractive than Aristotle's. When the western empire fell into the hands of heathen tribes it was the voice of a Platonist, St Augustine (AD 350–430), the greatest Latin theological writer of the era, that rallied the Church, inspired missionaries to convert the heathen, and laid down the way western Christians were to think for a millennium.

In the Greek east Aristotle was remembered longer, and

when Islam conquered those territories Plato and Aristotle were studied in Arabic. In Muslim Spain, in the century before Aquinas, Ibn Roschd (Averroes) (1126–98) wrote famous Arabic commentaries on Aristotle, and soon, in Spain and Sicily, both Aristotle and Averroes were being translated into Latin. Aquinas would have read them first at Naples, and learned even more when, having become a Dominican friar, he studied at Cologne under an Aristotelian scholar, Albert the Great. When he was called to teach in the university of Paris, he experienced the growing Platonic–Aristotelian struggle at first hand, especially when, at the age of thirty, he was given a chair of theology. The Augustinian theological faculty was fighting the Aristotelian novelties, which propounded a world eternal and uncreated, an autonomous human knowledge built on observation and logical reasoning rather than on inner illumination from God, a moral framework based on training in social virtues and pursued for happiness's sake rather than deriving from the Ten Commandments, and a certain scepticism about the immortality of the soul. In the year Aquinas was awarded his chair the arts faculty publicly espoused Aristotle, so that the theologian Aquinas found himself ranged with these philosophers against members of his own faculty.

Some people have described what Aquinas thereafter did in his short life as a reconciling of Platonism and Aristotelianism. I think it was far more radical. Aquinas never abandoned his criticism of Platonism, never abandoned his Aristotelian position, but he uncovered within Aristotle's emphasis on this-worldly individual existence and agency a far more potent pointer to God than Plato's emphasis on the other-worldliness of spirit. In Aquinas's view nature does not play second fiddle to supernature: God is in fact not supernatural but the source and author and end of the natural. For this reason Aquinas believed human reason has its own natural autonomy given it by God and respected by divine revelation; secular natural philosophy and sacred revealed theology must collaborate to build truth, aiming at harmony, not discord.

It is not too much to claim that Aquinas's views redefined the relation of the sacred and the secular, and helped to change the history of western society. The Augustinian and Platonic tradition continued to emphasize God's direct illumination of the soul and the distracting tendencies of the flesh, but even within the Church it now had a rival. And outside, secular reason began to exercise its muscle. Within 400 years of Aquinas's death Newton's mechanics had brought modern science to birth, resurrecting the early Greek atomists. The debate swung the other way when the philosopher Descartes, who accepted a sheerly mechanical conception of body, resurrected the Platonic view of mind as pure spirit – what the philosopher Gilbert Ryle was to describe as a 'ghost in the machine'. Three hundred years later Darwin would mount a challenge both to Descartes's view of mind outside matter, and to the Bible's view of the material world.

The two positions are still in conflict today, with a confrontation between religion and science of alarming proportions. The secular mind has found in big bang cosmology and evolutionary biology keys to understanding the material development and structure of the universe such as human beings have never had before. Religious establishments, their sacred texts disregarded, have responded with fury. Increasingly militant fundamentalist and authoritarian appeals to a God who apparently disregards reason have in their turn enraged and alarmed even moderate scientific opinion. Aquinas would surely have recognized the same struggle of secular and sacred, reason and revelation, material atomism and Platonic reality, in which he was embroiled. Aquinas's Aristotelianism may be just the refreshing view we need to resolve this contemporary debate.

In twenty-five years of working life Aquinas wrote over eight million words: two million of Bible commentary, a million of commentary on Aristotle, and the remainder divided into records of his university teaching and large compendia of theology for student use. The largest of these works read like an internet encyclopedia. Aquinas wrote discrete articles like web-pages, each with its own topic, linked to and referencing other pages to be consulted in parallel. From thousands of these pages I have selected nine extracts to illustrate how Aquinas thinks of the material world, how human reason can fit God in, how individuals and society are called to play God in a certain sense, what goes wrong with this in human history, and how the following of Jesus Christ can bring new light and new hope.

In translating the passages I have tried to be faithful to Aquinas's Latin, but I have not hesitated to transpose Aquinas's terminology and imagery into my own. The French philosopher Bergson, speaking to a gathering of historians of philosophy at Bologna in 1911, understood that behind a thinker's theses as they interact with one another and with those of contemporaries lie root images and conceptions driving the thinking. 'And sometimes not so much an image as a little push or breath of wind, a little dust-devil that reveals its own shape only by sweeping up into the air the dust and debris of the opinions of his time.' To understand Aquinas we must identify that little whirlwind and let it loose on the dust of our own time so that we can re-discern the shape of it in action.

FORM

First we ask whether the appearances under which mind knows things are drawn from the things themselves.

It doesn't seem so

[1]for Augustine says *bodies don't form images in our spirit; our spirit does that itself with amazing quickness*; **but** it wouldn't form the images if it got them from things outside; **so** the appearances under which mind knows things aren't drawn from the things themselves.

[2]Moreover, only the creator who gives a body its spatial dimensions can extract them from it; **but** anything taken into mind from things would have to have its spatial dimensions extracted from it (since it occupies space outside, but not inside, especially not in understanding); **so** mind can't draw appearances out of anything we sense.

However, this seems to contradict everything the philosophers teach: namely, that our understanding draws from our imagination, our imagination from our senses, and our senses from the things we sense.

My reply is that the human mind takes in from things the likenesses by which it knows them in the way anything acted on, any patient, 'takes in' something from the agent that acts on it. What it takes in is not some material element of the agent, but a likeness of the agent generated in the patient by the agent actualizing some potential the patient already has. This, for example, is the way our seeing takes in the colour of a coloured body.

However, there are different sorts of agents and patients. Some agents [a] are powerful enough to generate forms in patients all by themselves (fire by itself is sufficient to heat things), but some [b] can't do it without the help of other agents (heat nourishes only when acting as a tool of a primary agent – the animal's nutritive powers). Likewise some patients [c] don't cooperate at all with their agent (stones thrown upwards, for example, or wood being shaped into a bench), while others [d] do (stones dropped downwards, and human bodies taking medicine).

So this gives us three ways in which outside things relate to different potentials of mind:

- To our external senses they relate as [a] self-sufficient agents acting on [c] receptive but non-cooperative patients. (That colour needs light's help to act on our sight doesn't invalidate what we're saying, since light and colour both count as outside things; and although the external senses, once formed, exercise their own special operation of discerning their own special objects, the formation was taken in passively from things without active cooperation.)

- To our power of imagination also external things relate as [a] self-sufficient agents (for the agency of things sensed doesn't stop at our external senses, but extends to our inner powers of imaginative visualization). Imagination, however, is [d] a patient that cooperates with its agent in its own formation (for by combining and separating likenesses of things our senses have experienced, it forms for itself likenesses of things they have never experienced: having seen gold and seen mountains, for example, we can imagine mountains of gold).

- But to our potential to understand, external things relate as *[b]* non-sufficient agents. For although their agency doesn't stop even at the imagination but by means of the images formed there goes on to affect our potential to understand, that agency is no longer self-sufficient: for images as such are only potentially understandable, whereas our understanding needs objects that are actually understandable. It follows then that our receptive potential for understanding needs help from an agent understanding that can light up images and make them actually understandable in the way physical light makes colours actually visible. Thus the primary agency producing likenesses of things in our receptive understanding is clearly our agent understanding, though it uses images taken in from things outside as its tools. Also, receptive understanding (even more than imagination) is *[d]* a patient that cooperates in its formation by things, able to form a conception of what a thing is even when the thing cannot be sensed.

Hence

To 1: I reply that if by 'spirit' Augustine means understanding, then indeed it is not things primarily that form likenesses of themselves in the receptive understanding, but our agent understanding. If, however, imagination is meant then things themselves do act on our imagination, even though imagination cooperates, as we have said. But things need no help to imprint their likenesses on our senses. Augustine, however, wasn't talking of them, since he opposes sense to spirit and bodily to spiritual vision.

To 2: I reply that this argument talks as though an appearance
was some material entity moving across from a thing through
its image into our understanding, where it had to lose its spatial dimensions; but this picture is clearly false.

Quodlibet 8.2.1

At the age of thirty Aquinas was appointed to a chair of theology in Paris. During his seminars he would dispute questions
with his students and the records of such 'disputed questions'
form an important part of his published writings. Twice a
year, in accordance with the university's traditions, the professor Aquinas disputed questions in public, on subjects
chosen not by himself but by his audience. Such questions
were called 'quodlibets'. They have the conventional structure
of a disputed question, marked out by the words in bold.
First, the question is posed; then, at 'It doesn't seem so', come
edited remnants of the main arguments from the floor opposing the professor's position. On the day, these would have
been fielded by a graduate assistant. The arguments are cast
conventionally in loose syllogistic form, meaning they argue a
point ('S is not P', say,) by inserting a so-called middle or
stepping-stone predicate 'M' (asserting that 'S, *being M,* is not
P'). The text fleshes this out formulaically as 'S is M; but M
is not P; so S is not P'. After these arguments the word
'However' (*sed contra* in Latin) introduces arguments or quo-
tations of authorities that support the professor. 'My reply'
then gives the professor's solution, and 'Hence' introduces his
one-by-one replies to the opening opponents' arguments. All
this was recorded by a secretary, and edited later by the professor for publication by the university.

In the extract above Aquinas has been challenged to defend
an opinion that ranges him with the philosophers of the arts

faculty rather than with his colleagues in the faculty of theology: the Aristotelian opinion that humans derive their knowledge through their bodily senses from the material world outside rather than (as the followers of Augustine and Plato believed) by a divine illumination interior to their spiritual souls. It was a lifelong opinion of Aquinas. Question 10 article 6 of his *Disputed Questions on Truth* (*de Veritate*), the record of a seminar contemporary with this quodlibet, argues the same topic in much more detail with eight objections, three *sed contra*s, and a reply three times as long. Later in life we find him arguing it again in his encyclopedia for students, the *Summa Theologiae* (1a 84.1 and 1a 84.6). In these parallel passages Aquinas recalls the original classical Greek context of the debate, with Aristotle treading a middle path between the 'spiritualism' of Plato and the downright 'materialism' of an early Greek scientist-philosopher Demokritos (460–370 BCE). Demokritos thought the world a chance collection of atoms of matter in continual motion and change, in flux, never stable enough to be known with certainty – as Herakleitos (536–475 BCE) had put it, a river into which one could never step twice. Objection 2 and its answer at 'Hence . . . to 2', together with the first paragraph of the 'My reply', are meant to distance Aquinas from Demokritos.

Demokritos's materialist atomism is largely taken for granted today among the secular-minded: mind is a function of the brain (as digestion is a function of the stomach) and the brain is a machine the operations of which all 'boil down to a matter of atoms and molecules' (as brain-scientist Susan Greenfield put it in her TV documentary on the subject). Aristotle's middle path holds that nothing in our so-called material world is purely matter as Demokritos would have it, and nothing purely spirit as Plato would have it, for in matter

there is another element Aristotle calls 'form', and that is
what Plato mistook for a spiritual soul. For Aristotle, matter
and form are not two separate entities but two factors that
mingle together in a single entity.

Consider, for a moment, the skilled swimmer. She has
hands and feet and eyes and lungs – the potential to be a
swimmer. To this potential she has added a skill, by learning
how to coordinate her bodily parts into a certain kind of successful whole – a skill which has actualized her potential.
Without the actual skill there would be no swimmer, but the
skill is a realization of a bodily potential, actuality and potentiality united in the one swimmer's existence. Compare this to
the existence of any animal. It is a skilled survivor, made up of
cells and tissues and organs, and these of atoms and molecules,
all giving it the bodily potential of an animal. In each animal
the flux of atoms and molecules has been coordinated into a
certain kind of successful whole, actualizing that potential. A
particular skill has been acquired – the skill of surviving, of
existing in a way particular to that animal and preserving that
way of existing amid the ongoing flux of the world. Aristotle
calls this skill the animal's form, and sees it to be, like a skill in
swimming, an actualizing of a bodily potential. Actuality and
potentiality, matter and form, body and soul are not separate
entities but joined factors, matter giving the animal potential
and form actualizing that potential, endowing the animal with
its own particular ability to survive.

Our modern materialist atomism, like Demokritos's, also
describes the world as a flux of atomic events, appealing to the
findings of modern physics and chemistry. We must balance
this with what modern biology has to say about the coordi-
nation of those atomic events into stable surviving wholes
like plants and animals, the forming of the material flux into

the familiar ordinary world of things in interaction with each other within which we ourselves survive. Maybe every thing can be boiled down to atoms and molecules, but things are always more than what they boil down to; there is also in a thing what it adds up to, the form its matter takes on. A button's form, for example, is its function – its interface with the outside world of shirts and needle and thread. That function (whereby it holds together two pieces of material) cannot exist as an entity separate from the materials of the button, wood or plastic, but neither is it just another material part of the button. Rather it is the 'form' which actualizes the constituent material elements that are potentially button into something that actually is a button.

We can generalize these remarks to cover all machines. Here the matter is a machine's inner 'works', the structure of constituent mechanisms carefully engineered to coincide end-to-end with one another, the output terminal of one mechanism feeding the input terminal of the next. The form of this matter is the overall function those mechanisms implement when connected – the 'work' that the 'works' do which gives the machine its role and presence in the outside world. This outer function unifies the inner coincidences of many mechanisms into one identity, bicycle or VCR or airbus. Without such an identity a VCR would be just another heap of electronic junk, wired and wheeled and slotted to no purpose, unable to do anything. Each part of it might have a form, but there would be no form to the whole. What unifies and identifies the machine is the function its matter adds up to, and to this it owes its very existence, since it is only because of this wanted function that the machine is brought to be.

We might perhaps be tempted to say that we ourselves

impose on the button and the VCR the functions they have. But this is a little shallow: we think up these entities, it is true, but we don't pretend their functions. When thought up, they really do serve our purposes and are as real as those purposes. In any case, the argument won't wash with natural organisms like badgers and robins: we don't think up their role at all but read it in their behaviour. Natural organisms are in one sense machines and in another sense not. They have 'organized' insides, with 'organs' like stomach and brain (the word 'organ' comes from the Greek word for 'work' and means a tool or working part) and we can boil down these organs to atoms and molecules unified by the function they add up to. And the whole natural organism too has an external role that its innards add up to – not however in this case a function it serves, for no organism serves a function in the outside world. But it does have a unity or identity or presence hosted by its environment. It has a form to which the organism owes its existence and stability, its ability and skill to survive the hostility and thrive on the favour of its natural environment. Artificial machines exist because they are wanted by human beings to serve human purposes, but natural organisms are naturally selected to survive by the success of their ancestors.

So much then for Demokritos. But our discursus on Aristotle and matter and form is intended not only to illuminate what is wrong with the atomistic materialism underlying Objection 2, but also to prepare for Aquinas's rejection of the Platonic spiritualism of Objection 1. Indeed, Aquinas often starts 'My reply' with a survey of what we must have under our belts before we can satisfactorily tackle the question being disputed. Our extract hasn't room for an extended discursus, but the first paragraph of the 'My reply' – moving from seeing outside things affecting our minds as material flux, to seeing it as also interaction between formed things – is a relic of such a discursus, which we find much expanded in parallel passages. Now we must see how it illuminates what is wrong with the Platonic Objection 1.

Plato had been led by the mathematics of Pythagoras (569–475 BCE) and the ethical teaching of Socrates (470–399 BCE) to reflect on the eternal stability and certainty of certain truths, such as the properties of triangles and the virtuousness of justice. Ideas like these transcended Demokritos's unstable perpetually changing flux: the idea of a triangle had a perfection and completeness pencil drawings could only approximate to and human justice was an ideal that far outstripped actual human behaviour in which justice and injustice existed side by side. Plato grounded the intelligibility of such ideas not in the material world but in an ideal other-world of stable immaterial Forms, dimly and unstably echoed and reflected in the material world, like a radio broadcast suffering from bad reception. Human beings derived their ideas of justice not by sensing the imperfect material things outside, but by bringing to light the immaterial world of ideas within their spiritual souls.

This same dualist or two-world backlash against materialism occurred again in the sixteenth century, long after Aquinas's time. The philosopher Descartes, who thought animals mere machines, argued that mind, since it could not derive its certainties from animal experience, must, though tied to the body, be a totally different kind of substance. It is a view attractive to adherents of religion, western and eastern, providing an other-worldly place in which divinity and spirit can stand aloof and separate from the material flux, especially in an age in which Darwin seems to have demonstrated that human bodies are simply one branch of the animal evolutionary tree.

Aristotle's form in matter (he uses the Greek words for 'shape' in 'stuff') removes any need for Plato's immaterial Forms (he uses the Greek words for a form as an object of seeing or understanding). In Aristotle's world the mind is a form shaping matter rather than a conduit into the immaterial; it is a skill or ability we have to let the forms which shape the matter around us shape us also. For Aquinas and Aristotle a form is not a ghostly 'supernatural' presence *inside* a machine or organism, but the very natural overt and obvious presence *of* the whole machine or organism *to* what is outside it, its skill in independently existing in that world. The Latin word for the form of a living organism is *anima* – that which animates the plant or animal, actualizes it, forms it and gives it its claim to exist. Animals, as their very name suggests, have *anima* in a different mode from plants, a form bringing with it the skills of sensing, imagining and understanding. *Anima* is usually translated into English as 'soul', but in the extract above I have translated it as 'mind'; to have translated it as 'soul' would have distracted a modern reader, giving a wrong impression from the outset, making her think of some ghostly constituent entity within the body with a spiritual, occult presence of its own.

For Aristotle and Aquinas even an animal's mind is not some special entity or mechanism present *within* its body, but the special way in which its animal body is present to the outside world and skilled to exist stably within it, if only for a time between birth and death. That special animal way of existing is marked by an awareness of its environment and an expectancy and readiness to react to environmental changes that we might call the animal's 'stance' towards the world. Both Aristotle and Aquinas call it the animal's imagination, its 'picturing' of the world, but what they mean is rather its feel for the world. In the extract above Aquinas is maintaining that this animal-stance towards the outside world is nurtured by the things that inhabit that outside world acting on the animal's senses, but he is also pointing out that the animal has the ability to cooperate with the way things act on it.

So, in his 'My reply', Aquinas substitutes for the Demokritos picture of matter as a chaotic flow of atomic events an Aristotelian picture of matter as a process in which things with self-identity organize and disorganize. We as animals are organized in such a way that we can 'pick up' on the organization of the things outside us. Stably formed bodies in the outside world act on our stably formed bodies and our bodies cooperate with theirs, and this is the beginning of what we call knowledge. Knowledge builds up stage by stage, summarized in the 'However' of our extract. Our outer senses are so formed that they are totally patient and open to the forms that operate on them from the outside world; our imagination – our animal bodily 'stance' to the world it senses – reads out from things the significance they have for our survival as animals, and our human understanding illuminates its animal 'stance' with judgements about the objective roles such outside things play in the universe as a whole. For humans read not just what the objects of the outside world mean for our bodily survival, but also what their significance is in the whole scheme of the universe – what they indeed are. Just as physical light illuminates the colours of things but doesn't create them, so too the light Aquinas and Aristotle call the agent mind illuminates the objects with which sense and imagination have provided it, but doesn't create them. It brings to light their forms, and those illuminated forms are received into the receptive human mind as concepts.

In Paris in 1256 Aquinas's views were an immense upheaval: a new young theologian was taking the side of the upstart Parisian philosophers against his theologian colleagues, preferring to the venerable Augustinian and Platonic tradition of the soul as a natural inhabitant of a spiritual other-world the upstart Aristotelian notion of soul as the natural presence in this material world of a particular sort of animal body.

2

KNOWING

Next we ask how virtues like charity are known to people who lack them . . .

My reply is that knowing charity can mean (a) knowing *what* it is, and (b) knowing whether it is (by perceiving it in oneself, for example).

Now people can (a) know *what* charity is whether they have it or not, since human understanding is by nature made for grasping what things are, and goes about it in the same sort of way as it draws true conclusions about things. For present in us by nature are certain initial truths everyone knows, in which lie potentially known conclusions our reasons can draw out and make actually known, either [1] discovering them ourselves or [2] learning them from others or [3] having God reveal them, all of which ways of knowing rely on naturally known principles. When we [1] discover or [2] learn, these principles, filled out by sense-experience and imagination, suffice for acquiring knowledge; but even when they don't [3], they point us towards what is consistent with themselves; for human understanding is no more able to accept something inconsistent with naturally known principles than it is able to reject the principles themselves.

In the same way certain conceptions everyone knows are present by nature in our understanding: being, being one, being good, and so on. And from these our understanding draws out knowledge of what some particular thing is in the same way it draws out conclusions from self-evident principles. Again this happens either [1] by way of our own sense-experience (as when I use sense-experience of a thing's properties to form a concept of what it is), or [2] by hearsay (as when someone who doesn't know what music is hears that there is a craft which can teach one how to sing and play instruments, and, knowing already what a craft is and what singing is, forms a concept of what music is), or even [3] by revelation, as happens in matters of faith. For when we believe God has given us a gift of being united to him in affection we form a concept of what charity is, understanding it to be the gift whereby God unites us to himself in affection; for we already know what giving and affection and union are, having analysed them into things more primitively known; and so we go on until we come to those initial conceptions of human understanding known to everyone by nature.

Now the concept of charity our understanding forms in this way is not just a likeness of charity in the way a representation of something sensed or imagined would be; for our imagination and senses grasp only the outer properties of things, not their natures, so that what is represented in sense and imagination is not the nature of a man, say, but only the kind of outer properties a statue of him could represent. Understanding, however, grasps the very substance and nature of things, so that what is represented in understanding is a likeness of a thing's very essence; indeed it is in a fashion what the thing is, existing as understood rather than as it exists in nature in the thing itself. Whatever then cannot be sensed and imagined but only understood is known by its substance, what it is, existing somehow in our understanding. And this is the way charity is known for what it is, both by those who have charity and those who don't.

As to (b) knowing charity by perceiving it, Aristotle makes it clear that to perceive any ability or virtue (including charity) our understanding must perceive it in action. Now virtuous actions (acts of charity, say,) issue from the virtue in question as it really exists in its own nature, so knowing ourselves to have a virtue in this way is to know it by its substance existing in nature and not merely in our understanding. But only people possessing charity can know it in this way, for charitable and virtuous action is primarily an interior movement known only to the person acting; people lacking charity can infer other people to have it only if overt action makes the interior movement publicly perceptible. (In what I say I am supposing that a person acting *can* know his own charity, though actually I think this untrue; graced and natural love are so alike that even when acts are charitable they can't be sufficiently perceived to have issued from charity) . . .

Quodlibet 8.2.2

This is the 'My reply' section of a companion quodlibet to that of the previous chapter. There Aquinas discussed how things outside us act on our minds to reproduce their forms there. But according to Aquinas, this forming of our passive mind by things is not itself knowledge, but only a necessary preliminary to a mental activity which really *is* knowledge. The grammar of the verb 'to know' already suggests that knowing is an action (the subject 'knows' in the active voice), but it also suggests that the thing known suffers that action (the object 'is known' in the passive voice). Aquinas believes the grammar is misleading. Only physical activities, like heating or hitting, go out from their agent to actualize potentials of something else; activities like knowing and loving stay in their agent to realize potentials of the agent itself. 'Our mind doesn't relate to what it understands as an agent to a patient,' he says elsewhere, 'but mind and known object together make up one agent . . . The operation of understanding doesn't travel between the person understanding and what he understands; it issues from both conjoined.' 'Knowing as such does not produce an external effect; it interiorly perfects the knower in the way existing perfects what exists: just as existing is actually having one's own form, so knowing is actually having the form of what one knows.' Mind and object together exercise a shared presence in and with one another, a mutual indwelling in which the outside physical presentation of the object plays a part in its mental representation. Here the word 'representation' needs to be properly understood as 're-presentation'. A thing's presence outside the mind, able to make a material impression on other things, is re-conceived, re-presented, as a significant presence, and so is enabled, by its significance, to make a non-material impression on the mind itself. Let us illuminate the situation by comparing it with seeing things.

Seeing brings a stone's material presence not into my eye but into *sight*, where 'sight' is the name given to the functioning of my eye; sight does not dwell inside me spatially as my eyeball does, but dwells outside me as a field of sight, stretching as far as I can see. When I say something is in sight I don't mean it is in my eye, nor do I mean that it has ceased to exist outside; rather its presence outside is what is now in sight. Compare the phrase 'in mind' with the phrase 'in sight'. When Aquinas says knowing is a conjoint activity of mind and some object taken into the mind, he does not mean the object is no longer outside the mind; on the contrary, it is the outside presence of the object that is in the mind, and knowing is the conjoint activity of the thing being present outside and the mind knowing (re-presenting) it as such. Existing is possessing one's own presence in the world; knowing is possessing another's presence in the world re-presented within one's own actuality of presence.

All this is presupposed in our extract, where Aquinas is replying to questions about how we know and recognize virtues we don't possess. For the moment think of virtue as a bias of the human being towards acting well (a bias of the human spirit if you are an Augustinian), a bias such as kindness or courage. In the part of the quodlibet omitted from this extract, a member of the audience has asked why, if virtue is already present in substance inside the virtuous spirit, such a person would need it re-presented in order to know it. Only the non-virtuous would need such a stand-in representation. A quotation from Augustine sharpens the problem: charity, it says, is so unique in substance that no representation of it is possible. Presumably then the non-virtuous can't possibly know what the virtuous are talking about. But Aquinas no more equates presence in the spirit with being in mind, than he equates presence in the body with being in sight. Virtuous and non-virtuous alike must represent virtue to their minds if they are to know it. Neither the virtuous nor the non-virtuous can conceive what it is, wherever it is, except by representing it in mind.

Let us compare and contrast the situation with that of any other animal – something Aquinas does implicitly in the paragraphs of his 'My reply' marked (a). Animals perceive presence through touch. All material things are in contact with the things next to them in space, but only animals can feel this space as something within and without them, changing from within to without just at the point where they touch other bodies. Feeling is mysterious: feeling the warmth of a contacted body is something more than being warmed by it. A pebble can be warmed by the warmth of my hand, but does not feel it. But when my hand is warmed by a pebble, it feels the warmth of the pebble. Aristotle talks of a kind of immateriality here – a taking in of a form without taking on its matter. Taking in a colour is not taking it on – you don't become tinged with that colour. All sensing of things by animals builds on this simple feeling of contact, Aquinas thinks, mediated or unmediated. Baby animals serve an apprenticeship learning to ascribe initially amorphous sensations of sight, hearing, taste and smell to parts of a spatial world into which they can walk and exercise their sense of touch. They build up their own complex 'stance' towards the world they touch, which Aquinas after Aristotle rather feebly calls their 'imagination' or 'picturing' of it. Imagination is built up not only from seen images, but from everything animals perceive with their senses; and the whole is filled out into a comprehensive faculty of touch that presents an animal not with a picture to look at but with a three-dimensional world to walk into, to occupy, and in which to take a stance.

The human brings to its animal stance what Aquinas calls 'understanding': an awareness of the objective presence of things. There is a sense in which animals are only abstractly present to things: they are aware of them only in their relevance to the animal itself. But underlying all human language and science is an awareness of a relevance of things to everything else in the universe, an awareness of their objective existence. Only humans have this concept of a universe in which things are objectively relevant. An animal picks up on outside presences relevant to its own stance in the world, its interface with its own environment; but a human picks up on that environment itself, knowing it to be contained within an expanding nest of environments stretching out to a universe, the ultimate environment. We don't need to have perfected our conception of *what* that universal environment is (and we have a far better conception of it than Aquinas had) to perceive in principle that it is there, just as a man who perceives that something is stopping the bathroom door from opening may, when asked what, answer, 'I don't know what, but something is.'

Touch then, filled out with sense and imagination, is the foundation of our perception of 'existence', on which is built our intelligence. Stones are in contact with the space around them but not alive to it; plants are alive to outside conditions but not to outside objects; animals are alive to outside objects but not to their objective roles in the universe as a whole; and humans are alive to the presence of things not only as they touch our own stance in the world and trigger emotional expression, but as they exist in the whole universe and trigger expression and articulation in the medium of public language, whenever we ask whether and what something really is. An animal can puzzle over something, as did a little dog which carefully watched me pushing my shopping trolley, head cocked, nervousness in its stance. 'I am perceiving it but do I know what it is?' he seemed to say. Because he does not have public language he could not enquire, either of me or of himself, 'What is this?' He could be puzzled as to what the trolley portended for him, how to react to it with his repertoire of responses. But to be really puzzled by what a thing is, in the scheme of the universe, we need the infinite possibilities of human language.

Aquinas stresses that though intelligence starts us on the route of knowing what a thing is, it only starts us – it knows what things are only in principle. Our intellect knows immediately that something is stopping the bathroom door from opening, but what it is needs filling out with argument and experience. In the extract above, in the paragraphs marked (a), Aquinas explores the way human beings use their animal grasp of things, combined with the experience of others communicated by a shared language, to elaborate our initial intellectual perception *that* a thing is into a conception of *what* it is. The dog may be content when experience has told it what to expect and what not to expect of shopping trolleys, but we want to go beyond this – to get clear what makes a shopping trolley a shopping trolley. What identifies it, what gives it its selfhood and stability in the world, what gives it its claim to be a part of that world, to exist? What is it about a shopping trolley, what is it about a dog, that, in the midst of so much hostility, finds overall if temporary favour with the universe?

When we ask such questions we are ordering our animal observations into three sorts of statement about a thing: firstly, statements which define and identify, generically or specifically, what makes a thing an existent self; secondly, merely factual statements which happen to be true of it but are not implied in its definition; and thirdly, a collection of rule statements 'proper' to it, accompanying its definition and deducible from it, laying down what factual statements about it would make sense, whether they happen to be true of it or not. Aquinas, following in Aristotle's footsteps, thought the proper business of a science was to define its subject's natural place in the universe, and from that definition deduce rules laying down what facts could be true of the subject. He did not think he could deduce the facts themselves – that needed observation – but he thought he could deduce limits to what could sensibly be said about things. His science was more what we would call philosophy, and it took place not in laboratories or in the field, but in the debating halls where he tried to find sense in the world. Nevertheless, the starting point was the observed nature of things. And, as we read in this extract, even the revelation of God had to observe the rules that the nature of things laid down. Aquinas's faith might lead him to accept certain facts about the world the truth of which he could not deduce naturally, but even such facts must make sense to natural reason. If they didn't they could not be facts about the world. Thus it became part of the theologian's task to use his natural reason to show how revealed truths might make sense.

Part (a) of the extract explores this scientific process, concluding that what virtue is is determinable by the virtuous and the non-virtuous alike, deducing its definition and properties from the normal tools of observation and the word of others. This is a quite different approach from that of Augustine, who believed he could, by introspection, enter into immaterial 'contact' with the virtue in his own spirit and 'taste' its substance, so to speak. Aquinas thinks this is a covert appeal to divine illumination, avoiding the hard work of proper human investigation, but he is polite. Augustine might have been meaning, he suggests, that mental representations do represent the 'inner' substance of things and not merely its 'outer' properties, but he knew that that was not what Augustine meant. Augustine meant that a divinely given perception of virtue could substitute for a scientific conception of it, but Aquinas is defending the necessity of human science.

In part (b) Aquinas turns from the question of how we conceive what a virtue is, to the question of how we perceive that it exists, in ourselves or others. Again he takes a strongly Aristotelian and un-Augustinian line: we conceive with our minds, but we perceive primarily with our senses, not with our minds. 'Contact' and 'taste' belong to the material world. We perceive our own mental activities only when we recognize that our perception of the material outside world depends on us, on our position in space, on our education by others. So we perceive our own activities indirectly as the presence those things have in our representations of them; and even more indirectly we perceive possession of virtues and vices by perceiving the biases we or others display in those activities. But this is now perception tinged with conception and we can make mistakes, priding ourself on having a sort of love we don't really have, as Aquinas notes. In passages parallel to the extract we have chosen Aquinas goes on to consider self-perception – perception of the one subject in whom all our biases and activities are integrated. This is even more prone to mistakes: we can see *that* something exists which we call ourselves, but *what* are we? Perception of self needs proper conception of self: the perception has to be filled out with scientific study of ourselves and of our effects on the outside world, and that, Aquinas says, is hard work. Aquinas does not believe that human beings have any inner private hot-line to self-knowledge.

Aquinas's religion therefore does not depend on some supernatural perception of supernatural entities, in the way that many secular thinkers today think religion must depend.

Even our own virtue is not directly perceptible to us. It is part of our interpretation of the world we perceive with our senses. Aquinas was not interested in some enchanted world beyond science's powers of disenchantment. He was interested in pressing more and more deeply into a scientific account of the natural; already in that world there were things which only his religion would be able to explain.

3

EXISTING

[a] . . . When an agent stops acting its imprint persists in the effect only if it has taken root there, in the effect's nature. Thus the form and properties genetic to a thing persist in it till it dies having been made part of its nature, just as habits are hard to change because they have become second nature; but other dispositions and movements of body or soul outlast their agent's action only while en route to some natural state. And any effect which surpasses the nature of what it affects won't outlast its agent's action at all – light doesn't hang around in the air when the lamp is taken away. So, since existing belongs to no created thing's essential nature but only to God's, if God stopped acting nothing would go on existing . . .

Summa contra Gentiles 3.65

[b] People sometimes find it hard to understand how works of nature can be ascribed both to God and to natural causes:

[1]For it seems one activity can't have two agents; if the activity producing a work of nature belongs to some natural cause it can't also belong to God.

2 Again, when one agent is enough to do something, more than one is superfluous: we don't see nature using two tools when one will do. So if God's power is enough to produce a work of nature, having a natural cause produce it would be superfluous, or if a natural cause is enough to produce an effect on its own, having God do it would be superfluous.

3 Moreover, if God produces the whole of some work of nature there is nothing left for natural causes to do.

So it seems one can't say God and natural causes produce the same effects.

But in the light of what we have already said, these points present no difficulty:

1 For in any agent there are two things to consider: the thing acting (fire, say,) and the quality empowering it to act (heat). Now the power of a lower agent depends on that of higher agents, which either give it its power or maintain it or put it to use in the way any workman puts to use a tool appropriate to his work, a tool he didn't make or maintain but only wields. So a lower agent's action issues not only from its own power but from that of all the higher agents, since it acts in the power of them all. The thing most immediate to the action that produces the effect will be the lowest agent, but the power most immediate to the action will be the highest agent's power; for the lower agent's power to produce the effect comes not immediately from itself but mediately from the power of the next agent up, and that from a power higher up still, so that only the highest agent's power is immediately and from itself productive of the effect (as we see also in proofs where only the first premises are immediate). So it is no odder for a single work of nature to be produced by a lower agent and God than it is for a single action to be produced by an agent and its power, and to be produced by each immediately, though in different ways.

[2] Clearly too, even when a natural cause is producing an effect proper to it, there is no superfluousness in God too producing it, since the natural cause only produces it by God's power. Nor is it superfluous if works of nature, all of which God could produce by himself, have their own natural causes. This is not due to some inadequacy in God's power but to his immeasurable goodness which wills to give things the gift of resembling him not only in existing but also in causing other things, the two ways all creatures in general resemble God. Moreover, in this way creation is endowed with the beauty of order.

[3] Clearly too, the same effect is not ascribed to a natural cause and to divine power as though part came from God and part from the natural cause; the whole comes from each in different ways, just as what we do using a tool is wholly the work of the tool and wholly the work of the tool's user.

Summa contra Gentiles 3.70

In 1259 Aquinas was thirty-four, and had recently finished a busy three-year stint as a Paris professor. Back in the Italy he left as a novice Dominican friar fourteen years earlier, he was assigned to the priory of Orvieto to train a new generation of young friars, and finish a book begun in Paris that we know as the *Summa contra Gentiles.* The literal translation is *Compendium against unbelievers*, but the early manuscript editions called it *A book on the truth of the Catholic faith against the errors of unbelievers*. Most of the work's four volumes, housed in the Vatican library, still exist in autograph manuscript, its ink changing in the middle of Volume 1 from Paris ink to Italian ink. The many corrections and rewritings show what great trouble he took over the work. In some ways it is his most personal book in form, matter and intention.

Unlike the works written for classroom use, which record or mimic the form of classroom disputations, this work divides into chapters (though, as in extract [b] above, these sometimes adopt the disputation format of objections, exposition and replies). Theology is treated in a new way, designed to appeal to the human reason of 'Gentiles', by which Aquinas means Muslims and pagans – people who did not accept the authority of the Christian scriptures but would respect reason. In his first three volumes Aquinas restricts himself to matters he thinks reason can prove true (that nature and a God don't mutually exclude one another, for example), expounding his proofs first and quoting Christian authorities only at chapter ends to show that what has been proved is indeed what Christians say. In his fourth volume he turns to matters which reason can't prove true but can defend (that God has a son who became a man, for example). Scholars argue as to whether Aquinas was really addressing this *Summa* to Gentiles; in my opinion he was addressing it to himself, having decided the relationship of reason to faith needed facing up to, with justice done to the autonomy of reason. In the quodlibet quoted in Chapter 2 he maintained that even when, as in matters of faith, the principles of natural reason don't suffice to give us knowledge, 'they point us towards what is consistent with themselves; for human understanding is no more able to accept something inconsistent with naturally known principles than it is able to reject the principles themselves'; and in another quodlibet later in life he says that when disputing questions in theology, a master must use reason to explore the root of truths: quoting naked authority declares a thing certain but gives no shred of understanding of how it is true, and sends students away with empty heads.

The two extracts above are taken from the third volume of Aquinas's *Summa contra Gentiles*. In the first volume he has reasoned that a God exists, and in the second argued that God causes the existence of everything else. The third volume treats, in 163 chapters, of the prudence or providence with which God looks after the well-being of what he has created, and our two extracts from that volume combine to make one point: that God acts in the world through natural causes, so that God's agency and the agency of natural causes are not alternative agencies but related to one another like the agency of a workman and that of his tools.

The medieval cosmological system made this analogy seem simpler than it is. The world of material flux, organizing and disorganizing into temporary stable things, was confined in that system to the part of the world within the orbit of the moon. Outside the moon were things exempt from the flux, that could not decompose: the incorruptible eternal spheres of the sun and the planets and the stars, placed within one another like the layers of an onion, rotating with movements that stirred up the sublunar flux and caused the ordered and cyclical changes that took place within it. And God could be pictured as the cause of the outermost rotation and so of every natural motion and change within. This cosmological system however is dead and gone, demolished between Aquinas's time and ours by two great scientific revolutions.

The first, under Galileo and Newton, took the earth (the part of the world in flux) out from the centre of the revolving heavens (the part of the world exempt from flux) and reconfigured it as just one of many planets revolving round one of many stars. The second, under the geologists and Darwin, aided and abetted now by the theory of the expanding universe, destroyed the notion of everlasting species determined top-down by the agency of the spheres, and made of nature a contingent order emerging bottom-up throughout a long history of evolution. Yet strangely the second revolution has restored to us a way of interpreting Aquinas that the first revolution had destroyed. For in one sense, Newton did not so much take earth's flux out into the heavens as bring the heavens' exemption from flux down to earth: Newton's mechanics, which brought the two together, was a mechanics of hard, massy, impenetrable particles that did not decompose, following the same geometrical rules that everlastingly governed the heavens. Matter became infected with a mathematical incorruptibility. Animal bodies became machines, and God was seen as their engineer. Darwin's revolution, on the other hand, firmly returned the world to biological corruptibility, and in so doing preserved the idiosyncratic variety and unpredictable individuality of its living forms. The fact that his ideas so fitted how nature was increasingly seen to have developed helped astronomers to see that the heavens too had evolved bottom-up in the most idiosyncratic and surprising ways. Darwinism demolished the top-down medieval cosmology Aquinas took for granted, but has liberated us to see another aspect of Aquinas's work: a bottom-up metaphysics of existence in which God is in immediate presence to every individual part of nature, caused or uncaused, more interior to things, as he says, than the things are to themselves.

The world we now live in is, it seems to me, philosophically nearer to Aquinas than it is to Newton. It is characteristic of Aquinas's metaphysics to make more of existence (of what he calls *esse*) than it makes of form. In Aristotle's metaphysics it is form which gives existence, actualizing things which are only potentially in matter, and agents act by drawing out form from matter. But Aquinas is interested in the notion that form cannot claim to cause existence *per se*, of its own nature. Aquinas, you might say, almost 'defines' God as the source of this connection of form with existence. His is the agency which connects the two.

Time and again Aquinas makes this point in different ways. The extract marked **[a]**, for example, makes the point by saying that *esse* (existence) surpasses the nature or form of any created thing, which means that nothing in that nature says that it has to exist; if then that nature brings with it existence whenever the universe allows matter to take it on, then it must be that God (who is his own existence) is lending a likeness of himself to the thing coming to be. Existence must be on loan from some source of existence, the extract says, in the same way as light is on loan from the lamp. This way of thinking about existence is suspect to many philosophers: light is a real property of things, whereas existence seems to be merely the logical notion of instantiation of a property. Such philosophers think that to say cats exist is not to point out a property of cats, but to point out that the property of being a cat is instantiated; to say there are three angles in a triangle is to say that the concept of angle is instantiated three times in a triangle. But in Aquinas's sense of existence cats exist in a way the angles of a triangle don't, because existing is surviving. To survive they must be favoured by their environment, and that in turn by a containing environment, and that, eventually, needs the favour of the ultimate environment that is the universe descended from the big bang. To exist is to enter into the universe's existence, to partake of the universe's reality and unity. Existence is not the least thing you can say about anything, what is left when you leave out all its real properties. Rather it is the most perfect thing you can say, since, as Aquinas remarks, even being a lion is no perfection unless you actually are a lion.

Aquinas's notion of existence has a certain absoluteness about it that can never be gainsaid; something that has been can never be said not to have been, even by God. That absoluteness comes from its position as a temporary centre favoured by the whole universe. Here 'the universe' is a construct for everything else in the world, thought of as the environment of this thing we are considering. But in order to give favour, everything else needs to have it. Only if there is somewhere an act of absolute favour that itself needs no favour, something that is existence itself, will the existence of eveything else make sense.

The relation between the act of absolute favour and the existence of anything is what Aquinas calls creation. He believes (with his Christian faith) that things all began in time, but adds (with his human reason) that even if they had existed for ever, they would still need at every moment the relation to God he calls creation. If God stopped favouring a thing, the thing would stop existing. The presence of anything declares the presence of God; 'God is operative in every operation of will and nature'. This is why extract [b] argues that God is not a superfluous addition to natural causes. Anything that causes something to exist does it by bringing a form into matter, and that needs the cooperation of God as the ultimate favouring environment for all forms.

Extract [b] also argues a point Aquinas thought important in opposition to certain Muslim theologians – those who said that it was not fire that heated but God that heated in the fire.

In other words, they thought that natural causes were super-fluous – God did everything immediately. Aquinas thought this showed less love for nature and the world than God himself showed. God wanted things to exist like he did, and be agents like he was. In fact things do not exist, Aquinas says, except to act. Not to see that creatures act is not to see that they exist, and that is not to see God in them, and that is not to see God at all.

Aquinas believes that God causes not only everything that is naturally caused, but also everything 'uncaused', by which he means chance events. Chance events are coincidences resulting from a crossing of two independent lines of causing. The fact that some article on Page 3 of a newspaper is back to back with some photograph on Page 4 can be a pure coincidence. Someone intended the article to be there on Page 3, someone intended the photograph to be there on Page 4, and as a result there they were back to back, but the back-to-backness was not intended. Even if the same person intended and caused the two separate placings, that doesn't entail that she caused the coincidence as such. Yet it exists and can have real consequences in the real world; such coincidences some-times count, and because they exist they are acts of God. God's favour doesn't have to be carried down a chain of nat-ural causes. He is immediately present to everything, even the places where two chains of natural causes coincide by sheer chance.

Whether then a thing occurs by chance or not is irrelevant to God's causality. Aquinas has a God that doesn't only act top-down, present to things mediately through designed and engineered arrangements of causes, but also acts bottom-up, present immediately to the thing as its ultimate favour. The medieval mindset did think that God and nature mainly acted top-down (though recognizing the bottom-up chance event as possible and occasional and rare: the gentically disordered 'monster', for example, that nature occasionally generated). Modern man is faced with a world in which chance plays a much larger part, but God is also acting. This is a point important to recognize when reading Aquinas. He would think any opposition on theological grounds to evolution by creationists and proponents of intelligent design thoroughly misconceived. Whether scientifically they got the world right or wrong, they would be getting God wrong. Creation is tied not to design but to *esse*. There is in the world *esse*, actualization, and it arises from potentiality for *esse*: the potentiality, thought of as passive, is nature, thought of as active, is God. God is, Aquinas says, the author of nature. God gives nature *esse*. And God is present wherever *esse* is present – on the surface of things, where they interface with the rest of the universe. God exists not far out in the heavens, not deep in the mechanics of anything, but on the surface where things themselves exist.

4

CHOOSING

It seems that non-rational animals choose

¹ For Aristotle defines choosing as *seeking in view of a goal*; but non-rational animals seek and act in view of goals; so non-rational animals choose.

² Moreover, to choose means to select one thing in preference to another; but non-rational animals do that (we see sheep eat one kind of grass and refuse another), so non-rational animals choose.

³ Moreover, Aristotle tells us that *prudence is an intelligent choosing of the best means to an end*; but non-rational animals exercise that sort of intelligence. Aristotle's *Metaphysics* talks of 'animals like bees, intelligent without having learnt to be, since they can't hear'; and we see for ourselves the wonderfully ingenious behaviour of animals like bees and spiders and dogs: a hound following a stag through a crossroads sniffs to see whether the stag took the first or second road, and finding it didn't takes the third without sniffing, as confidently as if it had argued by exclusion that since the stag did not take the first two ways and there are no others it must have taken the third. So non-rational animals, it seems, can choose.

However, Gregory of Nyssa says that *children and non-rational animals do what they want to do, but don't choose . . .*

My reply is that because choosing is preferring one thing to another it needs to have several possible alternatives to choose between; when everything is already completely determined no room is left for choice. Now the difference between sense-appetites and will is that sense-appetites are by nature fixed on particular objects, whereas will, though by nature determined to a general object (namely, whatever is good), is not fixed on any particular good. Choosing is peculiar to will then, not sense-appetites; and since sense-appetites are the only appetites non-rational animals have, they can't choose.

Hence

To 1: I reply that seeking in view of a goal is called choice only when one thing is preferred to another, and that can only happen when there are several possible things to want.

To 2: I reply that non-rational animals select one thing in preference to another when their wanting is fixed on that thing by nature. When an animal's senses or imagination are presented with something it is drawn to naturally it immediately pursues it without choosing, just as fire burns upwards, not downwards, without choosing.

To 3: I reply that change is, as Aristotle says, 'actualization of something potential of change by an agent of the change'. Change then displays its agent's power, so that, when reason is the agent, the things changed display the orderliness of reason even when they themselves are non-rational – an arrow shot by an archer makes straight for the target as if it knows where it is going. The same can be seen in the movements of clocks and other works of human engineering. Now artefacts are to human craftsmanship as natural things are to God's, so that nature, like reason, as Aristotle remarked, moves things in orderly ways. Some of the things non-rational animals do then seem ingenious, because their nature orders them to superbly ordered courses of action planned by the highest craftsmanship, and as a result we call certain animals intelligent or prudent. But this is not because they reason or choose, as is shown by the fact that all the members of a species act in the same way.

Summa Theologiae 1a2ae 13.2

This passage is an 'article' from Aquinas's greatest work, the *Summa Theologiae*, which he began writing for his Italian students in middle life. ('Article' is the name given to the smallest units of this work, all of which have the disputed question format.) While writing it Aquinas moved back from Italy to Paris for another three-year stint as a professor, and on his return taught students at Naples near his birthplace. Before he had finished the work, he died. The *Summa* is an immense theological course for students articulated out of very simply formatted disputed questions, each question having usually three objections and one *sed contra*, and a 'My reply' limited to one small topic.

The extract above makes a point about choice, noting that animals other than humans don't possess it. But we will see that Aquinas does not take the dualist position that humans are spiritual souls with free will and animals are material bodies without it. Just as he used Aristotle's analysis of things into matter and form to throw light on knowing, so too he uses it to throw light on choosing. Humans are animals with animal instincts and desires, but in humans the desires are subject to a further awareness of the objective nature and goodness of the things desired, and that gives humans a measure of control over them that other animals do not have.

Objection 1 questions this difference from other animals. All animals, it suggests, act with goals in view. Aquinas agrees and he goes further. All natural things seek goals, even when they don't have goals in view. All things in nature exist and act, are engaged in being and in doing. Within the ongoing world-process each of them achieves a temporary stability we call existing, with an identity favoured by its immediate environment. That identity becomes a factor in the way the world-process is handed on to other things. The existing thing becomes a participant in the ongoing process, appropriating it and making it its own to some extent so that it becomes an identifiable part of the favouring environment of other things. The existent thing becomes an acting thing, an agent, a secondary beginning of the process. Sulphuric acid, once formed, becomes the agent of corrosive changes that hydrogen, sulphur and oxygen could not have achieved independently; a tree once rooted changes the habitat beneath its shade. Because such things introduce new directions into the process, says Aquinas, they can be said to be *seeking* the furthering of the process – seeking goals. Natural movement is here being contrasted with forced movement. If anything is steered or inclined towards a target without that inclination in any sense beginning in it or belonging to it we will call the inclination 'violent'; but if the thing steered inherits from its agent some form or disposition by which the inclination becomes its own we will call the inclination 'natural', as if in some way its own nature began it. Natural things lead themselves, *seeking* that to which they are inclined spontaneously. 'That is why the book of Wisdom [8.1] says divine wisdom "disposes everything sweetly", ordering it to its goal *by a movement of its own* [*De Veritate* 22.1].'

So every natural thing seeks goals. But animals do more. They act 'in view of a goal'; they are aware of their goal as a goal. The natural thing's seeking is just the determinate inclination it has by nature to act in a way that suits it. It doesn't have to determine for itself whether the inclination is suitable: things with unsuitable inclinations get weeded out by the environment. Animal seeking, on the other hand, is an emotional sensibility seeking something because of its suitability, for reasons of usefulness or pleasure. Because of this the seeking is more the animal's own than natural seeking is, determined by what this particular animal is aware of. Animals exist and participate in the ongoing world-process at a deeper level than, say, plants: the seagull as it swoops down to the surface of the sea, skimming it within millimetres without touching it, then rising again and soaring above, is a different sort of *self* from the rose, reacting to the external conditions of the environment but unaware of the objects it contains. The seagull is an object moving among a world of objects, finding its place in that world, relating itself to other objects. Nevertheless, as Aquinas notes, when an animal recognizes something as useful or pleasurable, say when it sees prey, its reaction is fixed and determined by nature So this is still not the kind of self a human animal has.

Human inclinations also depend on awareness, but humans are aware of objects not only as useful or pleasurable but as having an objective identity, related to any and every other object, with a place in the objective scheme of things. Animal awareness has ready-made reactions tied to the perceived usefulness or pleasure of outside objects, but human beings can correct their reactions by reference to more universal and objective considerations. This objective human awareness arises within my sense awareness: within my emotional sensibility (telling me what the outside objects mean in my world), my rationality is telling me what my world means objectively in the real world. Our animal self is surrounded by an environment of objectivity which is our understanding mind. For just as sight is a susceptibility to light, so understanding, as Aristotle put it, is a susceptibility to being, a susceptibility to the objectivity of objects.

Aquinas's view then is that all agents aim at goals, but to different degrees. What is violently shot at a target passively obeys the agent that fires the shot; it in no way moves itself to the goal. But if something like a living plant has natural inclinations to a goal, then it can be said to move itself, but in ways fixed by nature; there are natural reasons for its movement but it is passively unaware of them. The inclinations of animals driven by awareness not only have reasons, but the animal directs itself according to those reasons, along determinate paths of reaction built in by the nature of the animal species. To these the individual animal is still passive. Only if the inclination follows on an awareness which can test the reasons and the paths of reaction against a concept of what a goal is, and what is objectively a good goal, do we have free inclination, human free will. Human beings are aware of a notion of goal. They are not only attracted to things by their senses, but can adopt the attractive thing as a goal or reject it. They are also aware of the way their activity relates to the goal, and so can construct their own reactions. Human action is in the fullest sense voluntary: humans deliberate about what appears attractive, think about what steps will lead to it and what the consequences will be, and decide whether to pursue it as a goal or not. Animal activity is voluntary in a lesser sense (once they are aware of the goal, they want it and pursue it without premeditation).

The focus of our attention has so far been on goals. Our extract, however, talks more about choosing. According to

Aquinas these concepts are related. Goals are what attract us to act, but they cannot be pursued except by way of some means of attaining them. The process of finding such a means Aquinas calls deliberation, the act of adopting it as a means he calls choosing, and the act of pursuing the goal by way of those means he calls intending. In pursuing a goal, then, we first deliberate about what actions would further it and which of those are available, a deliberation which terminates when it reaches a means we can adopt, something we can start to do here and now. If we find more than one possible thing to do then a good education needs to guide our deliberation towards the most suitable.

Deliberation is an operation of our reason. In Chapter 2 we saw that in speculative matters understanding an idea means understanding it in terms of earlier ideas, which in turn are understood in terms of yet earlier ideas, until we were driven back to naturally understood ideas. But we don't have to go back to scratch every time we understand something. Our reasons become educated and filled out as we progress in life. Similarly, in practical matters the deliberations of reason that make our will free need eventually to rest on a naturally under-stood concept of what a goal is, and a naturally willed acceptance of goodness. But we educate our reason and through that our will and through that our emotions so as to recognize a good goal by second nature, so to speak, without going back to our most primitive natural basis all the time. We educate our-selves to deduce good actions, so to speak, from a natural inclination of our wills to goodness that has previously been filled out by education.

Notice that for Aquinas even free will is in one sense deter-mined. By nature we tend to will whatever can present itself to our reason as good to pursue. To say will is free means firstly that no particular object can oblige us to *exercise* our will, for, whatever it is, we can always decide not to think about it and so not even present it to our will. Secondly, no worldly object can fully satisfy our will. If it could, then by nature we would be obliged to will that thing when it presented itself to us, and refuse its opposite. But there are very few *things* that are good from every point of view (in fact only one, God, and we don't know enough about God to realize that). There are *ideas* of things which are good from every point of view. Aquinas thinks happiness such an idea. By happiness he doesn't mean a feeling of happiness, he means fulfilment. We can't help willing fulfilment, he thinks. Indeed for him will means the desiring of fulfilment: to will *is* to will happiness. We find this difficult to grasp because we are used to thinking of will as willpower. For Aquinas will is not willpower, it is willweakness: it is a weakness or attraction for anything that fulfils, anything good, anything happy. But no particular good in this world can be regarded as good and happy in every respect, so we are always free to think of it as not good in some respect and for that reason we are free to refuse it.

However, we can approximate to a more determined and powerful will, one which though free by nature is determined by second nature. That is what we meant above by an 'educated will', and Aquinas thinks it a good thing only if the education is towards a second nature he calls moral virtue, and a bad thing if the education is towards moral vice. The Latin language talks of natural things having 'virtue': it is a word for 'fully realized potential', measured by stretching a potential to the ultimate it is capable of: the horse's virtue, for example, is the maximum speed it is capable of. How things attain to such virtue depends on what kind of potential we are considering.

Natural agents like sulphuric acid have virtue by nature, born, so to speak, disposed and prepared for life by mother nature. The sense-powers of humans and other animals develop due to the action of external things upon them. But there are abilities that have to act on themselves, that have to prepare themselves, before external objects can trigger them into action. We have to learn to appreciate certain music, for instance, before that music can affect us, or learn how to listen to people before we can hear what they say. The virtue of such abilities demands a filling out of the ability with stable dispositions (or *habits),* which, though they don't trigger immediate action, prepare an ability to act well when circumstances require it.

Humans, able to behave in more than one way, setting their own goals and choosing their own means of attaining them, can meet with sudden trying circumstances, and behaving well in such circumstances needs an ability disposed to behave well. Humans may by nature have an inclination to goodness in general (the will, as Aquinas understands it), but man has to learn by practice the best ways to realize that inclination faced with the particular goods of this life. Such practice is a self-parenting, aided by the community in which we live – a way of naturalizing good choices so that we produce in ourselves the second natures of good choice that Aquinas calls moral virtues.

Not all the dispositions that Aquinas calls virtues are moral virtues. Some dispositions help us to get something done correctly or incorrectly – crafts, for example, like grammar and the sciences. But some dispositions are moral virtues, helping to get the human doing of such things done well, according to the proper rules of choosing and deliberating, and preserving a right respect for goodness as such. These moral virtues put balance into our reason (what Aquinas calls prudence), balance into our actions towards others (justice), and balance into our emotional readiness to act (courage and moderation). Indeed, because these virtues, unlike crafts, perfect not things done but the human doing of them, Aquinas believes them to be all parts of one integrity, the submission of our life to reason. You can't have one without the others, he thinks; moral virtues all stand or fall together. They are, as Aquinas puts it, connected.

In our modern world Aquinas could be understood as follows. Newborn babies are subjected to a sensed world that bombards them. Gradually the desires and fears they experience build the structure of importance the world is going to have for them as animals. Part of that structure is species-decided (Aquinas calls it what they desire *naturally*), part of it individual decided (their *animal* desires) and part, in man, objectively decided (*rational* desire). This rational desire is what Aquinas means by will. At this level the child's animal desires and fears are themselves externalized in a way not open to an animal. The desires are experienced as something bombarding a new interior self, in the way the sensed world bombarded the newborn baby. The natural and animal loves of the individual are being assessed for their objective satisfactoriness. This is what defines the humanity of human beings (at least as an ideal). In humans there seems to exist a sort of objective dissatisfaction which takes notice of the imperfect ways in which built-in desires and fears achieve their objective, namely our own good. At that moment of taking notice we discover this new interior in ourselves, this human will towards a more integrated *unanimous* self. It is not merely that we wish to preserve our self by reorganizing the world outside us – this would be true of any developed animal. We also wish to reorganize our self satisfactorily, according to a sort of intent of a new and better self. And if that intent is truly objective then it must be conformed to the intent of the universe itself as I would author it if I were its author. This inevitably brings in the intent of the actual author of the universe, if there be one. It explains why in developed societies morals and religion seem to go hand in hand. For any religious person worthy of their god (given that their god is worthy of them) there must be an intent of God for the universe that can perhaps be revealed to them and which they can acknowledge, a love of God for the world which they will want to implement and so return.

5

HUMAN AUTONOMY

[1] No law is eternal, it seems . . .

My reply is that laws are nothing but decrees planned by the practical reason of a fully fledged society's governing authority. But, given that the world is ruled by divine providence, God's reason governs the whole society of the universe, and the plan of government he has as the authority of the universe has the character of law. And since everything God plans is planned in eternity, not in time . . . we have to call it an eternal law.

[2] We don't seem to have law in us by nature
for . . . [2] . . . human activity is not ordered to a goal by nature in the way natural instincts order the activities of non-rational creatures to goals; human beings act for goals reasoned out and willed . . .

My reply is that because law is a rule that measures behaviour, law exists in things in two ways: it exists in the ruler measuring and it exists in what is ruled and measured (for what is measured partakes of the measure that measures it). Now clearly everything subject to God's providence is ruled and measured by eternal law, partaking in that law in the sense that its inclinations to its own proper activities and goals are imprinted on it by that law. But among such things rational creatures are subject to divine providence in a more excellent way, taking part in providence itself, making provision for themselves and for others, so that they also take part in the very reasoning which inclines them naturally to their due activities and goals. It is this partaking in eternal law by rational creatures that we call 'law in us by nature' . . . Clearly then the law in us by nature is nothing else than the way rational creatures take part in eternal law.

Hence

To 2: I reply that every activity of reason and will springs from what is in us by nature: all reasoning is based on naturally known beginnings, all willing of means to goals derives from natural desire of our ultimate goal, and, in the same way, what first directs our activities to their goal must be a law in us by nature . . .

[3] It seems there are no human laws . . .

My reply is that laws are decrees of practical reason. Now theoretic and practical reason proceed in the same way, deriving conclusions from premises. We should expect then that just as theoretic reason derives from unprovable but naturally known premises the conclusions of the different sciences (knowledge not naturally imprinted on us but discovered by reason's hard work), so also from the decrees of the law in us by nature, as if from unprovable general premises, human reason will need to arrive at more particular arrangements of

things. Given that they observe the other conditions required
of a law, such particular arrangements produced by human
reason we call human laws . . .

Hence

To 1: I reply that human reason partakes in the decree of
God's reason not fully, but in its own imperfect way. Just as
our theoretic reason partakes in God's wisdom by nature,
knowing certain general premises but not properly every single
truth as God knows it, so our practical reason also partakes by
nature in his eternal law, directing us by certain general
decrees but not going into all the detail that God's law nevertheless contains. So human reason must go to work and lay
down particular applications of that law.

Summa Theologiae 1a2ae 91.1–3

These are extracts from three consecutive articles of the *Summa
Theologiae,* dealing with law. The context is interesting. We are
in the second volume of the *Summa,* dealing with the ethics of
human behaviour. Aquinas has spent the last 200 or so articles
discussing what he calls the inner sources of human action: our
abilities to reason and to will, and the educated strengthening
(or weakening) of those faculties to act well (or badly) – our
virtues and vices. That was the focus in the last chapter. Now
Aquinas turns to what he calls outside influences on human
behaviour. He mentions two: the devil tempting us to do evil,
and God stimulating us to do good, teaching us by law and
aiding us by grace. These are two quite unequal influences.
The devil is what we today often call a 'supernatural' entity,
meaning an extra-natural one like djinns and gnomes and
astrology and witchcraft – the stuff of fantasy literature.
Aquinas thinks such entities, though they may exist, are relatively insignificant ethically: being extra-natural they exist

outside and are unable to get inside our nature and our reason and our will, the true sources of human action and behaviour. God, however, is a different matter: if we were to call him 'supernatural' it would not be because he is extra-natural but because he is the author of nature itself, and so both inside and outside it. What is true of God is true of the means he uses: law is both inside and outside (the moral law within and society's laws without), and the graces and favours of God can be both interior inspirations and external events.

The above extracts focus on the insideness and outsideness of law. The first starts with Aquinas's famous definition of law: a decree of reason, applying to a fully formed society, planned and promulgated publicly by whoever has the authority to govern that society. Human beings are social by nature, not just biologically but politically. Living a good life is not just a matter of individuals behaving prudently for their own goals, but of citizens of political communities using a communal providence or prudence to plan cooperative behaviour towards a shared goal. Law is an organ of this communal pursuit of a common good, an organ of citizenship, which in Latin is the same word as civilization. Our concepts of citizenship are moulded by much later philosophers – the Italian philosopher Machiavelli, for example, and the English philosopher Hobbes, believing a state or city to be a contract of submission to a central authority forced on reluctant individuals self-interested by nature. Aquinas, like Aristotle, thought that was the way cities negotiated with one another to avoid war, but that within the city the aim of law was the self-fulfilment of its citizens. 'Otherwise law becomes a mere covenant, a guarantor of men's rights *against* one another, instead of a rule of life such as will educate its citizens in a common goodness and justice.' As a result Aquinas conceives the authority of law differently from Machiavelli and Hobbes. Authority is the same word as authorship, and the authorship of law comes not from how it is acquired (from power), but from how it is authored or put together (its reasonableness). 'The will of the prince', if it is not reasonable, is tyranny and lawlessness, says Aquinas, and such a prince's laws have no authority. Nor would the will of the people if it were not reasonable.

This throws light on how our three extracts are linked. They analyse how law is 'authored', seeing in it a partaking in the providence of God himself, its first author. The first extract says boldly that law is actually a name for God himself, like wisdom or goodness, words first met in speaking of human beings but then applied without metaphor to God himself. God is a God-law, an eternal law, and the eternal plan of God as the universe's communal providence directs it towards God as its communal goal. In the second extract we learn that if God is a law, so too are humans, having in ourselves what Aquinas calls 'natural law', the light of natural reason mirroring God-law. In fact, the translation 'natural law' is highly misleading. We use it in ordinary language for the laws of nature science uncovers. But Aquinas carefully distinguishes 'natural law' from laws of nature. God has written laws into the natural instincts of all creatures (call those 'natural laws'), but into our reasons he has written law-writing itself (so it might rather be called 'natural lawmaking'). Reason prescribes the first precept of all self-regulation and all enacted law, summarized by Aquinas as *Pursue good and avoid evil*; and from this primary precept, by reasoning about ourselves and the world, we derive many secondary consequential precepts. Enacted human laws form part of those secondary laws: as social beings living in communities with legally constituted authorities we make the primary precept more explicit for ourselves by means of more specific moral guidelines. Some of these guidelines ought to be explicit in all communities (Aquinas calls them 'the law of peoples' and we call them human rights), but there is also room for civil laws in which particular historical communities lay down their specific ways of implementing the general patterns that reason lays down in general. Specifications not in keeping with the patterns, not in accord with right reason, will not have the character and force of law, but are bad law, indeed are forms of lawlessness.

Aquinas's view of law then is that it derives its authority or authorship from God by the mediation of reason used autonomously by men. 'Natural law' is not a code of obligations and rights already written in our hearts in the way God writes into us our natural instincts; natural law is a code we must do the writing of, using the reason God provides. So in a way we, like God, are laws unto ourselves, but only when we plan according to reason. The Christian Churches have, to their credit, been guardians of Aquinas's concept of reasonableness as the criterion of law, but often they have used the concept of 'natural law' to limit the human autonomy it implies. Religious people, for example, faced with modern legislation on matters like abortion, cloning and euthanasia are prone to accuse the legislators of 'playing God'. But Aquinas's view of 'natural law' clearly *requires* human beings to play God. The question must be whether the legislators are playing God reasonably rather than arbitrarily, and this is not as easy to decide as many religious people think.

The content of 'natural law' is indeterminate in three different ways: first, it is not worked-out law but law in principle; secondly, it is an abstract formulation of concrete action; and thirdly, it objectifies matters which are often subjective. Let us examine these three points in turn. Firstly, natural law tells us where to begin and leaves the rest to us; it provides us not with a finished toolkit, but with the where-withal to make our own tools. *Pursue good and avoid evil* is a first principle – it contains only a beginning content (an artic-ulation of what goodness means in practice). Such a principle of action is filled out into concrete practices with the help of our own experience and the suggestions of others (including God), just as Chapter 2 said we build up theoretical conceptions of what things are (what music or charity is, for instance,) from an initial conception of what existence is. Such principles are however attitudes rather than statements, meant to be used rather than stated – the seeds of conclusions rather than standing out as conclusions themselves. *Pursue good and avoid evil* may be articulated in words, but what it states is some-thing inarticulately present in the nature of our reason and the nature of our will – an initial natural orientation and loy-alty to goodness.

So natural law is indeterminate in the way everything basic and primary to understanding is inarticulate, whether the understanding be of theory or practice. But there is a second indeterminacy, characteristic of practical matters. Reason directs practical behaviour by arguing towards actions. But actions, as soon as they cease to be merely proposed and become actually done, escape from every limited abstract horizon and enter into the unlimited concrete world; they become related to all other facts, all other done things, uncountable and immeasurable. In fact we 'play God' when-ever we act, because we give this immeasurable real existence to a product of our own reason, fiddling with the universe itself. That is a heavy responsibility – fiddling with the universe – and we give it the name 'moral responsibility'. How are we to know with certainty the universal concrete consequences of something we do? A change of circumstances can change the moral significance of an action totally. In speculative thought we aim at conclusions that have the same truth or rightness for everyone in every circumstance, but in practical matters there is no such rightness. That people should return what they borrow is right in most cases, but what if it is a returned gun and is about to be used on the next-door neighbour? Perhaps one thinks one can legislate for every circumstance separately? But, as Aquinas says, the more circumstances one writes into laws the more opportunities there are for loopholes. Practical thought is indeterminate, then, in this second sense that it fails in universality: there is no such thing as a course of action good in every circumstance that can be determined by law. Instead, with the educated skills we call 'virtue', we aim at what seems good in the circumstances here and now.

And there is a third indeterminacy. Human behaviour is not exhausted by external action; such action arises from interior emotions, from desires and fears. One can legislate to some extent for external actions – the sum owed is the sum to pay, and a gun borrowed is in most circumstances a gun to be returned – but we can't legislate for emotions. In Aristotle's words, we can measure the balance to be observed in matters of justice, but the balance to be observed in matters of emotion varies widely from temperament to temperament – what counts as courage and moderation in one person is not necessarily a good measure of courage and moderation in another.

There is then no escaping the duty of 'playing God', of using our reasons to work out in detail what things in general are good and bad (and this a large part of Aquinas's *Summa* goes on to do) and what things are good and bad in the continually changing circumstances of our lives (and this each of us has to do every day). In another article shortly after our extracts Aquinas gives an example of how experience can start filling out his principle that good must be pursued and evil avoided. Observe first, he says, what human beings naturally tend towards: like every body they aim at individual self-preservation, like every animal they aim at species-preservation by male-female pair-bonding and the bringing-up of children, and like everything with reason they aim at knowing truth and creating peaceable societies. Immediately one sees that filling out the detail of the natural law is fragilely dependent on what one has experienced and how one reasons from it. Would Aquinas be able to say today with such confidence that every animal aims at male-female pair-bonding and the bringing-up of children? And even if he could, would he find them all doing it the same way? Could he maintain that monogamous relations and married family life are laid down by natural law? Aquinas allows that individual self-preservation has its limits as a precept of natural law – that there are circumstances under which life may lawfully be taken and circumstances under which one may give one's life for another. May there not likewise be circumstances under which normal mating and education may be bypassed? May different societies not work out human nature in different ways? Raising such questions puts the concept of natural law in perspective – it is no short-circuit across natural reasoning, but precisely God's demand on man to use his own reasoning about what is right and wrong.

Appealing to natural law as a short cut has become common-place nowadays when the churches want to voice their opposition to what they see as sexual aberrations. So I want to consider two further points in this chapter: Aquinas's attitude to sex, and the claims to legislative authority by organized religion.

Aquinas discusses sex in several places: when he speculates on what happened in the garden of Eden, whether passion is the evil Stoic philosophers maintained (No!), whether chastity is a virtue (Yes!), whether taking a religious vow of continence can be legitimate (Yes!). Unlike some earlier (and indeed some later) theologians Aquinas has nothing against sexual pleasure. He rejects a tradition which connected the transmission of original sin from one human generation to another with unlawful enjoyment of the act of generation itself. He thinks it possible to pursue pleasure in the sexual act in an inordinate manner, but he does not mean (as Augustine apparently does) that the pleasure can be just too much, but that one must not make pleasure an excuse for acting in ways that would otherwise be unjust. He states that not only would an innocent Adam and Eve have practised intercourse in the garden of Eden (which some earlier Fathers of the Church had denied), and not only would they have enjoyed it, but, because of their sinless state, they would have got more pleasure out of it than their banished successors. And though he accepts that genital motions, like the beat of the heart, do not obey reason, and that the moment of intercourse tends to distract our mental attention, he will not accept that indulging in sex is therefore unreasonable. One might as well call going to sleep immoral, he says.

When we carefully study the passages in which he judges sexual sin severely, we find the severity is based not at all on distaste for pleasure or excess of pleasure, but on the consequent injustice that it can do to sexual partners. We wouldn't find it difficult to follow his arguments if we thought of rape or child pornography, but we live in societies where injustice to one's own or one's partner's spouse in adultery, or injustice to a virgin's family in fornication escapes attention. Aquinas does not discuss these matters when discussing justice but when discussing moderation of sensual desires; nevertheless, when defining different types of sexual sin, it is the different injustices they do that he appeals to, and, when assessing their relative gravity, he adopts as a criterion how much injustice they do. Pleasure, for Aquinas, is a good, but far from the only good, and not the most important.

Whatever else can be said of Aquinas he was not a prude. Was he, however, sexist? He inherited an inadequate biology: he repeats Aristotle's opinion that a female is a male *manqué*: human seed *intends* to produce males but due to unfavourable circumstances such as the dampness of the south wind occasionally produces females. But at this very point his innate reasonableness reminds us that whatever may be said of the human seed's intentions, the intentions of nature as a whole are clearly to produce as many women as men, and the fact that it is nature's intention means also that it is God's. He quotes Paul's statement that in the body of Christ – the new graced society ushered in by Christ – there is neither male nor female, meaning there can be no discrimination in regard to their Christian status. However, like Paul before him and modern popes after him, Aquinas belonged to his culture and time and believed that men and women have different roles in society; only men, for example, can teach openly in church, though he adds that women anyway do all the teaching of the children in the home. Aquinas was a man who disliked prejudice, and had a very fair mind, but he was a man, and a medieval man at that.

As to the claims and authority of organized religion, Aquinas believes religion to be natural to man, because he believes it to be natural to reason. The arguments that he deploys with great subtlety to prove the existence of God he believes to be

articulations of the way every human being makes sense of the
world in his heart. Just as we see the world first, and then ourselves in the world as the standpoint from which we are seeing
it, so he believes we become conscious of the world as
belonging to another standpoint before it belongs to ours. We
move about in the world in somewhat the same way as we
move about in someone else's house, noticing that we are
guests and someone else is the host. And so we are naturally
inclined, every now and again, to expressions of gratitude –
and that, he thinks, is religion. As part of the organization of
communities and cities and states, religion too is organized. It
has a special relationship to lawmaking, because it deals with
the recognition of the author of our lawmaking. But just as
knowing that we exist in the world is a long way from knowing what sort of thing we are, so perceiving God's presence is
a far cry from knowing what God is. Most attempts at organized religion make a complete hash of that. Ancient Israel is
his recognized exception: the prophets embarked on a programme of purifying the concept of what and who God was,
a programme intimately connected with authoritative claims
on the moral behaviour of Israelite men and women, and
especially on their kings and priests, their lawmakers. Ancient
Israel's human law – its particular way of filling out natural
law – gets the nearest to revealing God as he is. He is thinking of the Ten Commandments as a succinct expression of
natural law, and of the positive injunctions laid on the rich to
respect the rights of the poor, and on priests not to put ritual
and temple observances above mercy and loving kindness.
But with the coming of Jesus, Aquinas believes, even this law
was superseded. A New Law, written in the hearts of those
who follow the way of Jesus, supersedes the Old Law written
by Moses on tablets of stone. Aquinas believed the earthly

guardian of this New Law to be the organized Catholic Church with the Pope at its centre. Moral teaching and teaching about the natural law was one of that Church's duties, but Aquinas fairly clearly did not believe the Church with its pope was an alternative political organization with an alternative prince to the Holy Roman Emperor. Only in the city of God to come would there be one society and one prince with a law entirely spiritual in the hearts of all its citizens. In the meantime there were the different states, secular organizations called on to use their autonomous human reason to develop human laws out of the natural law for the pursuit of the common good.

DISORDER

The human body seems an unsuitable sort of body for understanding to ensoul

[1]for matter should be in proportion to its form; but understanding can't decompose; so it should not inform a body that can . . .

[4]Moreover, the more perfect a form the more perfect its material should be; but understanding is the most perfect life form of all; so, given that other animal bodies are naturally protected (clothed in hair and shod with hooves) and naturally armed with teeth, horns and claws, it seems understanding should not ensoul a less perfect body, deprived of all such aids.

However, Aristotle defines soul as *the actualization of a natural organized body capable of life.*

My reply is that because material serves form rather than form material, form must explain the character of its matter rather than vice versa. Now the human life form is the lowest grade of understanding in nature's hierarchy, not (like angels) born with knowledge of truth but gleaning it by sense-experience from things in space; so that nature – since it always provides what is necessary – must add to this life form's ability to understand an ability to sense, and, since that requires a bodily organ, the human life form must inform a body organized for sensing. All sensing, however, is based on touch, which requires an organ that strikes a balance between the opposing qualities it has to sense – not too hot, not too cold, not too dry, not too wet, and so on – so as to be able to detect and sense them. The more balanced its organ the finer its sense of touch will be; and since an intelligent life form needs the most developed ability to sense there is (higher forms carrying on where lower forms leave off), it needs to inform a body compounded of elements in the most balanced possible way. This is why human touch is more sensitive than touch in other animals, and the most sensitive among humans are the most intelligent: *tender flesh and a quick mind go together*, says Aristotle.

Hence

To 1: I reply one might hope to escape this objection by saying that before Adam's fall the human body couldn't decompose either. But this won't do: before the Fall Adam was immortal not by nature but by God's grace, otherwise he wouldn't have lost his immortality by sinning any more than the Devil did. So we must give another answer: that there are two sides to any material, one suiting the form for which it is chosen, and another its inevitable concomitants. Carpenters, for example, make their saws of iron because it can cut through hard things, but the inevitable consequence is that the saw's teeth blunt and rust. In the same way an intelligent life form needs a body of balanced composition, but the inevitable consequence is that it will decompose. If someone says God could avoid such inevitabilities, we answer with Augustine that when

we study the way things are in nature we must judge by what
suits this nature rather than by everything God is capable of.
In any case God in his grace has provided a remedy for
death . . .

To 4: I reply that intelligent life forms have universal awareness and consequently unlimited potential. As a result nature
can't provide for them a fixed repertoire of instinctive
responses, defence mechanisms and protective coverings of
the kind provided for animals whose awareness and potential
are limited in particular ways. Instead then nature gives us
reason and hands – those *tools of tools* – with which we can
make our own limitless toolbox for unlimited tasks.

Summa Theologiae 1a 76.5

So far we have been examining the order Aquinas finds in the
world. Within an ongoing flux there arise stable persistent
entities in interaction, each of them pursuing a story of its
own and helping turn flux into partially ordered process.
Outside the flux there is a God, a providence eternally plan-
ning a story for the process as a whole. Among the stable
entities there are human beings, unique in having a reason
which calls them to share in God's providence autonomously,
civilizing themselves and bringing order to the world in whatever ways seem best to them, 'playing God'. Now, in the
extract above, we meet the question of disorder for the first
time. If God and human beings strive for order where does
this disorder come from? Who is responsible? Is disorder in
the world God's fault or man's or both?

The *sed contra* reminds us of what Aquinas means by form
or soul: that which gives a stable entity its skill to survive and
not fall back into the flux, which gives it an actuality and existence of its own and saves it from decomposing. In human

beings it is an ability to reason and understand that does this. So our extract is asking whether the human body is well adapted for the successful survival of intelligence. Aquinas replies that a successful life of understanding requires the ability to assimilate how everything else exists, which presupposes imagination – an animal stance aware of the meaningful presence of other things, which presupposes the sense of touch, a refined ability to contact things and discriminate them. That is what the human body as constituted gives us, since 'nature always provides what's necessary'. For this last quote from Aristotle we could today substitute a quote from any elementary textbook on evolution, saying that if nature hadn't provided the necessary body, human being and human reason wouldn't be here.

Aquinas is here again opposing the Platonic and later Cartesian ideas that mind lives immaterially and body materially, and the two are wedded together in some sort of shotgun marriage. For Aquinas our understanding and our special sort of organ-provided body make up one nature, enjoy one natural presence in the world – a united presence which wins the favour of the immediate habitat, and beyond that the favour of the universe. Two sorts of activities cooperate in this one presence, mental and bodily, but there is only one thing there which is both bodily intelligence and intelligent body. The intelligence needs its body to be its organ of presence to the universe, as Aquinas makes clear in the 'My reply'; and, as he makes clear when answering Objection 4, the body needs its intelligence, to make absence of hooves and hair a virtue rather than a deficiency, and to make hands and reason good enough equipment to survive on.

The extract comes alive in Objection 1 and its reply. The objector suggests that understanding would have a much happier life if it could exist without the body, for under-standing does not of itself decompose in time. We see this, a medieval theologian could say, in the angels, which were thought to be pure intelligences existing for ever. The body introduces decomposition, death and pain – all the things our understanding revolts against. If our intelligence had to have a body could it not have been a better one, a non-decomposable one of the sort medieval science attributed to the sun and the stars? Perhaps indeed that was the sort of body God had given humans in the garden of Eden, and Adam (the Hebrew word for 'human being') had lost it for himself and for us by his original sin. Aquinas will not allow this escape. For him our intelligence needs its body, and death and decomposition, being natural deficiencies of bodies, are natural deficiencies of human beings. They are part of the nature of all matter, which can't get everything right at once: to all good there is attached natural evil. The same iron out of which it is good to make saws because it is hard, is also bad to make saws out of because it blunts and rusts. Aquinas's position raises then the question we now call the problem of evil – how do a good creator (God) and the evil in his creation go together?

It is not only matter that brings concomitant disorder and evil. Aquinas recognizes as the first great distinction within creation not spirit and matter, but good and evil. If the world has a creator, then existence is a contingent gift and a favour, not something things have of themselves. So it is something that creatures may lose, wholly or partially. By ranking the dis-tinction of good and evil as fundamental, Aquinas is acknowledging the force of what he called the greatest heresy of his time – the Albigensian or Manichaean heresy. Saint Dominic, the founder of the Order of Preachers, the religious order to which Aquinas belonged, had spent a great part of his life preaching against this heresy around Albi in the south of France. For the Albigensians, matter and material things, like having children, were evil. Good and evil were created not in one creation but in two, by two different creators. Aquinas acknowledges that the distinction of good and evil is a fundamental one, but it is a created one; it is not a struggle in the divine world between two Gods. Aquinas says these heretic Albigensians are even more mistaken than pagans.

In his view good and bad divide as presence and absence, and the division is asymmetric. Badness is not real in the way presence is real but in the way absence is. Badness is like blindness, not like sight: it is lack of good in the way blindness is lack of sight. Fundamentally, just by existing, the world is good, but what exists can fall short of fullness. Things exist by surviving, by winning the favour of their environments and the universe, by 'looking good' to the universe; but, for Aquinas, there is no possibility of having all that good at once without any concomitant disharmony. The universe as a whole is in fact better for including some things which fall short of goodness by ceasing to survive: fire must consume air in order to burn, pandas eat bamboo, and a lion's good is an antelope's evil. There are ways of improving the situation so as to be more even-handed, but to have the universe without any of it is impossible. Nothing is evil by nature, nothing evil in relation to the whole scheme of the universe, but some things are evil in relation to a particular part of the universe, and even then that evil is the good of some other particular.

As well as natural evils – pain, death and sickness – there is moral evil, even if only in human beings. The braving of pain and the soft-pedalling of pleasure calls forth in human beings a greater good, the good of goodwill. We can all cooperate in goodwill, or not cooperate. Badwill, an absence of goodwill, is moral evil. For Aquinas, it is a rejection of the universe's centre – God's goodwill – and an attempt to substitute for goodwill our own will. Such culpable failures of goodwill are what the Christian tradition understands by sins – not defined by breaking of laws as in the Old Testament, but defined by failures to cooperate in good. It is culpable faults, not afflictions, which are the really destructive elements in the world; afflictions deprive us of particular goods and sometimes very essential particular goods, but mis-willing deprives us of goodness itself.

So why does God allow it? Moral evil is always caused by pursuit of a good, says Aquinas; it is never directly caused or willed as evil, but is tolerated as a concomitant by someone intent on a goal they consider good. But the balance is wrong: the immediate good accruing to the doer of the act is ranked higher than the evils to self and other people, to society and the world, that accompany the good. The profit accruing to the shareholders outweighs the harm to the consumer. The good accruing to the murderer outweighs the harm to his victim. Nevertheless, in seeking a good the doer commits an evil. How does that come about? Natural evil in things done or made results from natural defects in the doer or the material being worked on (which implies a defect in the agent not finding the right material). But moral defect does not come from a natural defect in the agent – any lack of ability as such. Indeed such lacks often excuse actions from moral culpability: the doer could not help herself, or did not know what she was doing. Moral defect is not a defect in ability, but a defect in the exercise of the ability, the acting of this action, an acting not subjected properly to the balance of reason. That lack of balance in our judgement is not in itself the moral fault, not until the moment the agent allows the action to go forward.

The moral evil is the agent's free importing of that lack of balance into the doing of the action at that moment. There is nothing wrong with the action itself as a natural action, and God indeed is causing it, giving it existence. But he is not causing the lack of order in it; the lack is a free creation by his free creature.

In Aquinas's view, as a consequence of causing world order and harmony God causes natural evils and afflictions. Not even divine omnipotence can create a finite world in which natural evils will not be a concomitant of good. Knowing this, God chose to create this world, so he can be held responsible for its natural evils. But if we had the omnipotence would we truly choose to destroy it because of those concomitant evils? Aquinas thinks we would not, and that therefore blaming God is not really on. The true course is to accept the world, and take on our own share of the responsibility. We could try taking on the task for which the Bible says Adam was created: to enter into the world as a garden to till it and to keep it. The human being was given reason and free will and the autonomy to plan order and make laws, in order to share the providence of God for creation. And this role of human beings in creation shows why the creator even allows moral evils. Allowing sin is an inevitable consequence of allowing freedom. Freedom is our ability to act not just as somebody else has designed us to act, but as we by our own reasoning and love direct ourselves to act. God allows this freedom into his creation, because his whole idea is to let the universe make itself from the bottom up, by producing human beings and having human beings of their own free will help the universe towards order. For Aquinas, of course, it was the corruptible part of the universe below the incorruptible heavenly spheres – the part of the universe called earth – that the human being was called upon to till and to keep. For us it will be the whole universe.

The Bible story that recounts Adam's call to till the garden also recounts how Adam chose to disregard God's own say in the matter: the story of Adam's fall. As a result Adam inherited sickness and death, hardship and hostilities, and a nature red in tooth and claw. In this story, as Aquinas recognized, natural deficiencies are clearly being laid at the door of a culpable person's moral act. In St Paul's New Testament interpretation of this story, and in St Augustine's use of that, connecting the universality of Adam's sin with the universal human need of Christian baptism, this moral culpability is then passed on to every human being. It becomes an original sin (by which is meant a sin incurred at every human being's origin, incurred by the very fact of being born). Aquinas points out that such a sin could not be personal to every human being – a personal sin must be a free personal action, which being born is not. But Aquinas thinks every human being's being born, and being born in a defective natural state, is something for which Adam was responsible. He had had the opportunity to accept something better. So we are not all *doing* sin but we are all busy being an act of sin.

Now that the garden of Eden is accepted as a myth and not a fact, and the biological notions on which Aquinas based his theory of the inheritance of original sin have been shown to be fatally flawed, is the whole of what Aquinas says in irredeemable disarray? Can one deduce what Aquinas would have said if he were alive today? I think we can. Aquinas would have pointed to the reason why St Paul adopted the interpretation of the Genesis story which Christians have inherited. Paul was saying something about Jesus and his death as saving not just individuals, but the destiny of the whole human race.

He was attempting to explain why the whole human race, without Jesus, would miss its target. What Paul and Aquinas thought they saw in the Adam story was a human action that made the naturally deficient state of humanity its own responsibility: God offered aid to help man cope from the beginning with his natural deficiencies, and man, in Adam, rejected it. The Adam story can no longer mean that. But could not a Christian believe that God offers the human race the garden of Paradise as a destiny – a destiny offered not at the beginning of the world but in Christ? And our attitude to Christ accepts or rejects, implicitly or explicitly, that destiny. History, one might say, in all too public a way rejected Christ; but history also, in Christianity, has accepted him. So that now in history there is a choice to be made: for Christ or for loss of Paradise? If we are not Christians, of course, we do not really have this destiny of Paradise problem, but only the problem of how to avoid evil and pursue good in the garden of the world in which both exist.

7

JESUS CHRIST

Christ it seems is not head of the human race

¹For a head is head only to the limbs of its own body; but unbelievers are in no way limbs of the Church, which according to Paul is *Christ's body*; so Christ is not head of all humanity.

²Moreover, Paul says *Christ handed himself over for the Church that he might present it to himself glorious, without spot or wrinkle or any such thing*; but even among believers there are many in whom the spots and wrinkles of sin are found; so Christ is not even head of all believers.

³Moreover, according to Paul the sacred rituals of the Old Law compare to Christ as *shadow to body*; but these are the rituals the Old Testament patriarchs observed in their day, *serving a copy and a shadow of heavenly things*; so they did not belong to Christ's body, and Christ is not head of all humanity.

However, Paul calls Christ *saviour of all men and especially of those who believe*; and John calls him *the expiation for our sins and not for ours only but also for those of the whole world*; but it is as their head that Christ saves men and expiates their sins; so Christ is head of the whole human race.

My reply is that the mystical body of the Church differs from our natural bodies inasmuch as the limbs of a natural body all exist at one and the same time whereas the limbs of the mystical body don't. They don't in their natural existence (since the body of the Church is made up of people from every period from the beginning of the world to its end), and they don't in their graced existence in God's favour (since at any one time some of the people existing are out of that favour but will enjoy it later, while some already enjoy it). So people can be accounted limbs of the mystical body actually or potentially, and some potential limbs will never become actual ones, while others will but in three stages: by faith, by charity in this life, and by enjoyment of the life to come.

So I reply that in general Christ is head of all humanity across the whole of history, but to different degrees: first and foremost he is head of those actually united to him in glory, secondly of those actually united to him in charity, thirdly of those actually united to him in faith, fourthly of those united to him potentially and not yet actually (though in God's predestination they will be eventually), fifthly of those united to him potentially who will never be so actually, such as those not predestined but now living in this world, who, on leaving this world, will cease to be even potential limbs of Christ.

Hence

To 1: I reply that unbelievers, though not actually in the Church, are potentially so – a potentiality grounded first and foremost in the power of Christ, which is enough to save all humanity, and secondly in their own freedom to choose.

To 2: I reply that a glorious Church, not having spot or wrinkle, is the ultimate goal to which we are being led by Christ's sufferings, but that will be at home in heaven, not on the way there on earth. On earth, as John says, *if we say we have no sin we deceive ourselves.* Nevertheless, those limbs of Christ actually united with him in charity lack some sins, namely fatal sins; and those tainted with such sins are limbs of Christ potentially, and perhaps actually in the imperfect qualified way in which loveless faith unites them to God. They are not united to him in the unqualified way which would enable them to live in grace through Christ, for as James says *faith without works is dead*; but they are receiving a certain act of life from him, namely believing, being moved around just as a dead limb can sometimes be.

To 3: I reply that the holy patriarchs used Old Law observances not for what they were in themselves, but as images and shadows of what was to come. Now, as Aristotle says, *reacting to an image as an image is reacting to the reality imaged*, so that these ancient patriarchs, by observing the ceremonies of the law, were borne towards Christ with the same faith and love with which we are borne towards him, and so belonged to the same body of the Church as we do.

Summa Theologiae 3a 8.3

Aquinas, in the third volume of his *Summa Theologiae*, inserts his understanding of the person and legacy of Jesus of Nazareth, the founder of Christianity, into his understanding of the cosmic process and the history of human being. The first volume of this work, 'on God and creation', he had written in 1265–8, while master of the Dominican study-house in Rome. The second volume, 'on the journey towards God of creatures endowed with reason', a vast compendium of human and Christian morals, had occupied him from 1269–72, throughout his second period as master of theology at the university of Paris. Now, at the age of forty-eight, he was again in Italy, in the area of his birth, master of his own Dominican study-house in Naples, the city where he had gone to university and where he had joined the Dominicans thirty years previously. Here he began the final volume of the *Summa*, 'on Christ who, as man, is our road to God'.

Though discussions in previous chapters have touched on God, these have been limited to what Aquinas thinks human reason can find out about God, to his philosophy of God, more often called his 'natural theology'. In this chapter we step into 'scriptural theology', a theology based on what God is revealing about himself in the sacred scriptures he has inspired men to write. Reason could not have worked out the truths revealed there, but, if we believe that the men who wrote the scriptures were truly inspired by God, it will be reasonable to believe what they say. Scriptural theology starts from such a faith, natural theology from observation of the world, but both theologies are exercises of human reason, exploring the implications of their respective starting points.

From the start the *Summa* expounds both natural and scriptural theology. Volume 1 discusses God as creator of the natural world, as we saw in Chapter 3, but adds a discussion of scriptural talk about the existence of three persons in one God, of the sort we shall see in Chapter 9. Volume 2 of the *Summa* explores a reason-based morality, but adds discussions of the specifically Christian 'virtues' of faith, hope and charity, and of Christian 'ways of life', like being a monk or a bishop. Because Aquinas was always scrupulous about distinguishing between faith and reason, we have been able to explore the latter without overmuch trespassing on the former. In this third volume of the *Summa*, however, Aquinas turns to what the scriptures have to say about Jesus, and we must therefore consider the Christian suppositions which underlie Aquinas's treatment.

The central supposition is that of 'grace', compared and contrasted with the concept of 'nature' we have been using so far. The word 'grace' is a scriptural word, the word 'nature' an Aristotelian one. Aquinas's scriptural theology brings the two words together, so that analogies with what Aristotle says about nature can be used to illuminate what scripture says about grace. When Aquinas first talks of grace in Volume 2 of the *Summa* he asks what the word signifies in ordinary human language. In common Latin speech, he says, it can mean 'benign favour', as in the good *graces* of a king; or a 'free gift' as when a *grace* is conferred *gratis*, or *gratitude* for such free gifts as when we say *grace* after meals. Gratitude presupposes gift, and gifts presuppose favour, so that the primary meaning of the word 'grace' is that of favour. But scripture is using the word to talk of some special favour from God, and that leads Aquinas to make two further comments. In ordinary human favour, some quality in the favour's recipient is first found pleasing and elicits the favour; then because of the favour the recipient receives a gift and displays gratitude. But when we come to God's grace, says Aquinas, since God is the source of all existence, his favour comes first and causes the recipient's pleasingness and the gifts received and the recipient's gratitude. Moreover, grace is not the first of God's favours; the very existence of things is a favour from God, the first of all favours.

Aquinas, following Aristotle, regards the form or nature of a thing as a skill it has for surviving in this world – a form favoured for existence by the ongoing world-process, and therefore by God. In this way of thinking 'nature' is a first grace, and grace itself a 'second nature' disposing us to a new kind of existence, that of being what the New Testament epistle of

St Peter calls 'consorts of God's nature'. Just as the favour of existence surrounds its recipients with an environment of contingent happenings and activities within which they are called to develop as knowing and lovingly disposed people, building up a happy community life for themselves and others, so grace, as a sharing in God's nature and existence, surrounds its recipients with happenings and activities and calls them to a knowing and loving communal happiness. Indeed it is the very same happenings and activities and human community that called us to earthly happiness by nature, that now call us by grace to happiness in this life and a life beyond it with God.

As a second nature grace brings with it a new set of virtues and vices, to be judged good or bad not so much by a balanced conformity to reason and natural law and a happy life on earth as by a 'deiformity', a conformity to God's life. These are the virtues of faith, hope and charity, which initiate us into a life in God's friendship, and a rebalancing of the moral virtues, so that they dispose us to live well in that friendship and earn an everlasting life beyond the grave. And, so the extract above maintains, just as nature, God's first favour, is mediated to us through the ongoing world-process, so grace, his second favour, is mediated to us through one man's life and the change he has made to history. Grace is conceived by Aquinas as a favour earned from God by Jesus's own personal living out of human life, and overflowing from there to the whole race to which Jesus belongs, to all human beings right back to Adam and forward to whatever end is in store for us all.

By asserting that the whole human race is called to share in the life of Jesus himself, scriptural theology is re-conceiving the whole of human history. History is being centred in a relatively recent event in its religious history, the event in which an Old Law for a specific nation (the law of ancient Israel, written in stone) was superseded by a New Law for all mankind written on the heart: Jesus in the Sermon on the Mount saying, for example, 'It was said to you of old . . . an eye for an eye, a tooth for a tooth . . . But *I* say to you . . . if anyone strikes you on the right cheek offer the other as well . . .' For Aquinas, the *I* of that saying is the *I* of a human being, and the call is a call to all human beings to identify with that human being, with that *I*. But the call is a call from God, because God in his grace has already identified with that *I*, with that human being, in the strictest sense of the word 'identify'.

Jesus is the first recipient of God's grace, at a threefold level. First there is what Aquinas calls the grace of union, the grace of being identified with God while remaining a true human being, a person one in nature and existence with God, a true Son of God the Father. That is unique to Jesus. Second there is the grace of being the most holy human being in his own personal life and a true friend of God. And third the grace to share the personal grace by which he is personally pleasing to God with all mankind, so that all human beings can become personally pleasing to God, made welcome to share God's friendship since they are friends of Jesus, his son. No one is excluded, every human person is a potential sharer. Jesus's grace will suffice if the person wants to be his friend.

The life with God and his son to which grace calls us is not a supernatural life, at least in the modern sense given to that word. It is not a different life from our natural earthly one, made up of abnormal happenings in some fantasy world. It is a deepened view of our ordinary human life, centring it on a relation to Jesus's human life, and centring that on a relation to the life of God himself. 'Grace does not substitute for nature but fulfils it,' says Aquinas. It is supernatural (more than natural) not in the sense of extra-natural (other than natural), still less in the sense of being un-natural or contra-natural, but in the sense of discovering a connaturalness to God in human nature, tapping a spring *within* human nature through which the ocean of God can pour, 'a spring welling up to eternal life' as Jesus calls it in the gospel of St John. Aquinas quotes a saying of Augustine that even if knowing and loving God face to face is impossible without God's grace, nevertheless to be *able* to know and love him is in man's nature; man is naturally able to receive this grace. In Jesus that grace was received, and handed on to all his friends; for, as Aristotle says, 'What is possible through friends is possible.' Grace is natural to human beings in the way tides are natural to the ocean, a natural effect in a natural object of a natural cause in an immediate natural relationship with that object. The ocean's nature is not exhausted by its internal physical and chemical constitution – it is also defined by its natural place on the earth's surface subject to the influences of sun and moon. The ocean cannot ebb and flow of itself, but its nature allows it to respond to its partners, sun and moon. In the same way, Aquinas says, the human being, because endowed with reason, is of its nature open to God, able to be moved by God to friendship, and disposed by God to a life of love in common with him; and the way God does this is through the personal life of Jesus of Nazareth.

Our extract distinguishes different links that human beings can have with the Jesus of history. The two most important are described as the virtues of faith and charity. Aquinas talks of these virtues as *contacting* God, through Jesus, and of bringing into our lives a new standard of behaviour – behaving as God would in our shoes. Natural moral virtues dispose us to actions which measure up to the standard of our own reason; the Christian virtues dispose us to embrace a further standard, that of God himself. Other virtues are virtues because of what they pursue: just or courageous or moderate acts. The 'theological' or deiform virtues of faith, hope and charity are virtues not because of what they pursue but because of why they pursue it. For it is an imperfection to believe *what* Christians believe without a proper motive for doing so – such faith is blind and blindness is an imperfection. But there is a virtue in believing a person who knows; and we all do it within proper limits, the limits of what that person knows. There are no limits to what God knows, so there can be virtue in believing *what* God says because of *who* is saying it. Even faith is lifeless in itself and no virtue: the demons, Aquinas thinks, can't help thinking it rational to believe in God but don't like doing so, and much good that does them. The life of faith is believing God as an act of love, loving him not as a *what* but as a *who*, with a love of friendship. Loving wine or horses, says Aquinas, is loving a what for having's sake, and if you think of God as a source of gifts solely for having's sake, that too is loving a what: it is not charity, the love of God as friend. Charity is loving God (in himself and in our neighbours) as a who, as someone to whom one wishes good for their sake, for giving's sake; and that shows itself in loving God and neighbour with the sort of love Jesus Christ had: 'No greater love has a man than that he lay down his life for his friends.' Only love of that sort can rescue faith from lifelessness and imperfection. Love when truly unselfish recommends itself. Only of such love can it be said, as Augustine is reported to have said, 'Love, and you may then do whatever you want.' This includes taking the risk of believing someone who loves in that way.

This brings us back to the difference between natural and scriptural theology, the first a reasoning based on nature as we observe it, the second a reasoning based on a belief in Jesus Christ as a way of life with which God has identified. In Aquinas natural theology is a part of physics and metaphysics. When exploring nature, process and existence, God comes across as a conclusion. Aquinas thought reason was bound to come across God in this way, though it could not conceive what God was in himself, merely perceive that he existed. Reason infers existence of causes from existence of effects, without always being able to infer the nature of the causes from the nature of the effects. Something is stopping the bathroom door from opening, but we haven't the slightest idea what. Aquinas thought natural religion arose not from observance of supernatural phenomena – he is relatively uninterested in miracles – but as recognition that the existence of nature itself had need of more cause than our science could ever supply. Aquinas thought being religious in this sense a virtue, but like all virtues it was a balancing between vices. On the one side lay the vice of too little religion – and our modern secularism would qualify as that. On the other lay the vice of too much religion which he calls 'superstition', but in which we might include all our modern fundamentalisms. For religion is not infallible and can easily make conceptual claims going far beyond the basic natural perception of the mystery of existence. Such claims can lead to error, mayhem and evil, especially when different ways of interpreting religion in different human communities lead to idolization of community identities. The history of religion is no different from the whole social history of man.

However, in Aquinas's view, Christianity is more than a natural religion. Jesus arose within the history of natural religion to turn that history around. Jesus's life was a self-revelatory act of God to a band of loyal friends and followers who knew him intimately, and who declared his identity to all the world. At the time Aquinas was writing the third volume of the *Summa* in Naples, he was also writing a commentary on the Gospel of St John. In that Gospel Jesus is identified with the word of God that opens the Old Testament, 'Let there be light!' In the beginning was the Word, says John – a commandment you had from the beginning, a commandment coming true in Jesus and us, his apostles, and you who listen to us; for the darkness is passing away, the word has become flesh and pitched its tent among us, and we have seen the glory of the only-begotten son of God and have touched him with our hands. The Law came through Moses, grace and truth through Jesus Christ; and we are announcing this to you so that you may have fellowship with us, no longer his servants but his friends.

This is the event which has turned natural religion into a life of faith and charity, and so turned theology from a learning of men into what Aquinas calls a teaching of God. Natural theology starts from natural existence as seen in the natural light of reason, and God turns up as a mysterious conclusion; but Christian scriptural theology is God's vision of himself passed on to us by the light of his revelation. That vision is not shared by us as vision but as belief, but that is the way the vision of all the sciences is shared by students when they are still learning. In the hope of attaining vision themselves some day they temporarily believe their teacher, because he has expertise and authority. Aquinas, we should remember, thinks of authority not as power to command blind obedience, but as a source of truth on which one can rely for eventual vision, in the way we think of Einstein as an authority on the theory of relativity. Theologians too, awaiting a promised vision of

God in the life to come, adhere in the meantime to articles of faith articulated by a teaching authority that already sees: God living in Christ.

Aquinas thinks of theology as a true science. It takes on faith scripture's articulations of the nature of God and his gifts, and treats them as premises of reasoning, in the way geometrical optics takes on faith premises from geometry. It is not the job of theology to prove its premises, any more than it is the job of geometrical optics to prove the geometrical theorems it applies. It is the job of theology to draw conclusions from the premises. In geometry *seeing* the truth of a conclusion reduces to *seeing* the truth of some premise, but in theology (and in geometrical optics) it is the *believing* of some conclusion that reduces to the *believing* of some premise. What we see is that something we don't see derives from some deeper thing we don't see. And we hope that in a life to come everything will be seen. Theology, then, for Aquinas, is a true science, based on a justified faith. His New Testament namesake, the apostle Thomas, on seeing Christ's wounds after his resurrection, said 'My Lord and My God!' Commenting on these words, Aquinas wrote: 'So is a sceptic turned into a good theologian.'

8

THE CHRISTIAN CHURCH

[a] Christ's suffering, as something willed by God, *effects* our salvation, as suffered willingly by Christ *earns* it, and as taking place in his flesh is an *amends* (freeing us from liability to punishment), a *ransom* (freeing us from slavery to sin itself), and a *sacrifice* (reconciling us to God).

Summa Theologiae 3a 48.6.3m

[b] Sacraments are tools for causing grace. For tools are of two types: separate like sticks and connected like hands, and the connected wield the separate as hands do sticks. Now God is grace's primary agent, with Christ's humanity as his connected tool and the sacraments as separate tools: power to save passes from Christ's godhead through his humanity into the sacraments. The graces the sacraments cause seem to have two main functions: firstly, to remove imperfection caused by past sins which though finished as actions leave behind penalties, and secondly, to perfect the soul to worship God through the religion of a Christian life. Now Christ freed us from our sins primarily by his sufferings, not only effectively but through earning and making amends; and with his suffer-

ings he also inaugurated the rite of the Christian religion, making himself an offering and a sacrifice to God . . . Clearly then the Church's sacraments derive their power especially from Christ's sufferings, to which the reception of the sacraments joins us in some way. And as a sign of this there flowed from Christ's side as he hung on the Cross water and blood, the water of baptism and the blood of the Eucharist, the two most powerful sacraments . . .

Summa Theologiae 3a 62.5

[c] In baptism we are incorporated into Christ's sufferings and death: as Paul says, *if we were put to death with Christ, we believe we shall come to life in him.* Clearly then every baptized person shares in Christ's suffering for their own healing as if they themselves had suffered and died. And since Christ's suffering makes amends for all mankind's sins, people baptized are freed from all liability to punishment for their sins just as if they themselves had made amends for all their sins . . .

The sin inherited [from Adam] was an infection passed first from Adam's person to all human nature and then from that nature to every person inheriting it. Christ, on the other hand, cures first what is personal to us and then afterwards human nature at one and the same time for all, which is why baptism immediately removes our inherited fault together with the punishment personal to us of not seeing God, but does not remove the natural defects of our present life – death, hunger, thirst and the like, which arise from natural causes and to which we have been abandoned by not having inherited rightness – until all nature is healed by final resurrection into glory.

Summa Theologiae 3a 69.2–3

At the time he wrote these passages on the Christian sacraments in the third volume of his *Summa Theologiae*, Aquinas was still at Naples; but one morning in December 1273, around the feast of St Nicholas, he fell into a great trance while celebrating Mass. Aquinas was apparently given to deep fits of distraction, but this one was severe, and from that moment, without explanation, he ceased his daily work on the *Summa* and spoke little. His secretary and friend Reginald of Piperno reported that after persistent questioning all Aquinas would say was that in comparison with what God had now revealed to him his writing seemed chaff. However, his wits were still intact. A month or two later he set out on a journey to Lyon in France for a council to which the Pope had summoned him, and as he passed the Abbey of Monte Cassino he sent them a letter they had solicited, explaining with great clarity how God can have knowledge of future events without compromising the contingent character of those events. A few days later near Teano – perhaps in another fit of distraction – he ran his head into the branch of a fallen tree and was injured. His health deteriorated rapidly, and he was taken to a Cistercian house nearby at Fossanova. Two weeks later, on 7 March 1274, at the age of forty-nine, he was dead.

The extracts above link two parts of the *Summa*'s third volume: the first extract comes from a discussion of what Aquinas calls the mysteries of Jesus as God's Word made flesh, and the last two from a discussion of what he calls the sacraments of the Church. There is a deliberate play on words here. In early Rome the 'sacred' was anything dedicated to the gods – temples, for example, and priests – and a 'sacrament' was a deposit or pledge made to the gods, and, derivatively, an oath of obligation sanctified by calling on the gods to witness it. The early Church used the word to translate the Greek *musterion*, a state secret, adopted by the so-called mystery religions to describe their secret rituals and teachings, and by the Christian scriptures to refer to God's eternal secrets finally revealed in Christ. By Aquinas's time sacraments most commonly meant those six or seven rituals of the Church like baptism and the Eucharistic remembrance of the Last Supper, believed to have been instituted by Christ as means of dispensing God's grace to the human race. Aquinas, however, shows himself conscious of the broader background. He first mentions sacraments alongside oaths in the second volume of the *Summa*, when he is dealing with religion as something natural to men. Sacraments are those rituals by which men externally acknowledge some gift received from God, in contrast with sacrifices – rituals in which men offer gifts to God. He is taking for granted that such symbolic gestures to God are natural to men, prescribed under the law we have in us by nature. But the particular form they take in any particular society will be specified by the humanly enacted laws and customs of that society. Israel was such a society, but one believed to have been specially chosen by God and consecrated to his worship. The laws laying down the form which sacraments and sacrifices took in Israel were deemed to have been enacted by the word of God himself speaking through Moses on Mount Sinai, instituting rituals attesting to the faith of Israel in a divinely promised future, a divine secret or *musterion*. Aquinas regards the sacraments of the Church as Christian successors to such specified rituals: actions of worship specified by Christ, attesting the faith of the community of Christian believers in God's gift already given in the mysteries of Christ's life, God's word made flesh.

But, for Aquinas, such rituals are not merely symbolic. They are also effective. He sees them as applying the results of

Christ's life – the redemption of the human race from sin and friendship with God – to those who take part in them. He sees them as channels of God's grace and, more daringly, as causes of that grace. The picture such phrases conjure up can mislead us. Aquinas does not picture grace as some sacred fluid supernaturally infused into interior veins of an elect. We have seen repeatedly that nature is not conceived by Aquinas as 'inside' a thing; rather it is the 'outside' of a thing in the sense that it defines the way the thing is present to its environment. Grace, for Aquinas, is a second nature, a sort of containing movement or pressure towards a further outcome to life. Grace is supernatural, more-than-nature, in the sense that it draws the whole of created nature towards union with God's nature. Grace moves us towards a friendship of natures, if one could so call it – a friendship in which created nature responds with freedom and spontaneity, initiative and autonomy to the overtures of a creator respectful of that autonomy and willing to cooperate with it. Aquinas's picture, as we saw in the last chapter, is of the ocean moving in ways more-than-natural under the influence of sun and moon.

As the first extract says, the causes of grace are firstly God and secondly Christ. But Aquinas sees the sacraments as tools of God and Christ in the spreading of grace, and in that sense also causes of it. A tool like an axe cooperates in the movement given to it by its primary agent, the human woodcutter, lending to the primary agent the gift of its own form (the axe's sharp edge). Of course, the axe has no autonomy, is not alive and cannot in any sense move itself. But human agents have autonomy, an autonomy given them by God; and when they move themselves autonomously, God is giving them that movement. So even the primary agency of human beings is secondary to God's agency, yet without losing its autonomy.

For such secondary 'primary agency' Aquinas uses the words 'meriting' or 'deserving' or 'earning'. These are ways of effectively bringing about a result which needs some other person's cooperation, ways of persuading that person to help achieve the result. So, in the first extract, and in the third volume of the *Summa* as a whole, Aquinas talks of Jesus, a free human being, lending his own earning, meriting, deserving cooperative work to the act of God forgiving and saving and putting wrong right, re-ordering a sinful human history. That work took place in Jesus's flesh, Aquinas says, by which he means that Jesus gave his historical life as a tool with which to earn God's grace for all history. And the culminating moment was his willing acceptance of an unjust death at the hands of opponents of his work.

Theologians have struggled to express how Christ's life, and especially his death, could have been a tool to win grace for mankind and forgive their sins. Aquinas quotes three of the ideas prevalent in his own time, pointing out that they are metaphors, dependent on what metaphors are being used to express the disorder Christ's life and death are putting right. If that disorder is pictured as a slavery – to the Devil, for example, or to sin – then Christ's gift will be pictured as a rescue or ransom. If the disorder is pictured as an offence – to God, for instance – Christ's gift is the act of a kinsman paying compensation and making amends. This is the picture contained in describing Christ as our redeemer, a word which comes from the Latin for 'paying back'. If the disorder is thought of as an alienation from God then Christ's gift is a sacrificial gift, offered as an earnest of the desire for reconciliation. None of the metaphors reaches the core of the matter. They raise the same doubts about the forgiveness of sin that Chapter 6 raised about the notion of incurring original sin in the first place.

How could Adam sin on behalf of the whole human race, and how could Jesus Christ win forgiveness for us all?

There is much in Aquinas's discussion that depends on an outmoded conception of how the human race started and how one generation influences another. But I think we can extract from it a theological view of Calvary and salvation without which Christian belief would have no point. The essential concept seems to be that Calvary is a bifurcation in human history. There are two ways for that history to go after Calvary: one leads to disaster for all humanity, and the other saves humanity from that disaster. Calvary was an event in which man confronted God and God man. At that point in history God put himself at the mercy of man, proposing himself as a source and wellspring of a new and everlasting life for humanity, offering it from within humanity. God offered himself as a head for the human race – not as a king but as a teacher of truth. The autonomy of the human race was accepted by God, so God had to allow himself to be either accepted or rejected by man. He was rejected; God was assigned to death. And just here an amazing turn of affairs takes place. For God accepted the rejection as a way of going on being present in the world for men – a way those who wanted to accept could accept, when and if they wanted, and a way those who wanted to reject could reject. God resurrected his proposal in a new guise, proposing himself as rejected for man's acceptance. From this point on men can choose between two histories: the normal natural history that will go on without heed of Calvary, and another graced history which will line up behind a God who has shown that though men can kill they can never prevent the dead from rising again.

That is the essential mystery of Christ, the divine secret hidden in his life. The events of Eden and temptation and loss of Paradise can be seen as a way of talking about Calvary itself, seen as the event in which God was publicly and politically rejected by human beings. The theology of redemption can be seen as another way of talking about it: as the event in which God and Christ responded to this public rejection, making of it something that individual human beings can accept and live through and employ as a tool for bringing reconciliation in this life and in the next. The primary tool is God's own human life, displaying the power of his love to remake creation, displaying it not by laying down a law or necessity on men, but by gambling on provoking a loving response. God is lord of chance, and on Calvary created a world which he will infallibly bring to fulfilment through the free actions of men.

This picture of Christ's life underlies Aquinas's theory of the sacraments. They are the further tools by which Christians can incorporate themselves into Christ's earning of salvation – incorporate themselves into the events of Calvary. It is as if, in Aquinas's striking phrase, those who take part in baptism go through Calvary themselves. (Aquinas here quotes St Paul, who said we 'dress ourselves' in the death and resurrection of Jesus, and invented new Greek words, saying that a baptized person has 'with-died' with Christ and will 'with-rise' with him.) The sacraments offer an 'edge' to Christ, as the axe offers one to the woodcutter. That edge is their ritual re-presentation of the events of Calvary. Aquinas says of them that 'they cause by signifying'. He does not mean merely that they represent, but that they *re*-present. They do not just picture symbolically, as pouring water symbolizes cleaning or as immersion symbolizes being buried with Christ. He means that they are actions joined invisibly by Christ's will to the action of his life and death – 'Do this,' he said, 'in memory of me' – and are actions that can be seen and touched. Just as in his life on earth Jesus was God seeable and touchable, so he is now in the sacraments. They are celebrations, full of mime and make-believe, which renew history day by day by reapplying the moment of history's bifurcation to those who take part in them.

For Aquinas, the seven sacraments recognized in his time by the Church are not really seven different tools of Christ's salvation. They are seven parts of one great ritual present in the Eucharist (nowadays often called the Mass). They are actions preparatory and consequent upon a ritual in which Christ himself is present. In the other rituals we see smearing of oil and pouring of water and hear people talking of what they are doing – visible signs of grace acting. In the ritual of the Eucharist we see bread and wine existing before us and hear a recitation of Christ at the Last Supper declaring what that bread and wine is – visible signs of Christ being with us. The materials present are in the form of food and are received as food. Eating food assimilates its substance and renews our natural life; eating the Eucharistic food symbolizes renewal of our graced life by assimilating the life of God in Christ. Natural food builds up our natural bodies; the Eucharistic food builds up the body of the Church, conceived of as the ongoing body of Christ and the ongoing body of God.

Aquinas also says that the Eucharist gives a special grace, a moment of actual love between God and the participant in the Eucharistic meal. It is like a daily kiss of God, renewing love and friendship, nourishing and building up the mystical or sacramental body of the Church as a community. Thoughts like the above, scattered in Aquinas's treatment of the Eucharist, are its theological backbone; though what has engaged readers over the centuries are his remarks on the

'miraculous' side of the Eucharist as the Middle Ages conceived it – the 'transubstantiation' of bread and wine into the
physical resurrected body and blood of Jesus. Aquinas argues
that if God in Jesus said of the bread at his last supper, 'This is
my body,' then his body was what it was, and it was bread no
longer. And if the priest at the Eucharist lends his voice to the
repetition of those words over bread on the altar, then from
that moment of consecration what is there is Christ's body,
and bread no longer. It appears to be bread but, 'miracu-
lously', what it is is Christ's flesh.

I personally think that the stress on 'miraculousness' is over-
done. In the century before Aquinas there had been a
spectacular controversy over whether Christ was 'really' or
only 'symbolically' present in the Eucharist. Aquinas's views
actually amount to a rejection of this dichotomy between real
and symbolic. The sacraments cause by signifying; what is
present is really present through a re-presentation. God's creation, taken totally, is larger than his material creation; Christ's
life and death has given our history a further, real significance. In this new history the ultimate significance of *this*
bread and wine in the Eucharistic celebration is more than the
ultimate significance of bread and wine in nature; and in
Aquinas's world we mean by the substance of something its
ultimate significance in God's universe. So there is a sense in
which the 'substance' of Christ's flesh and blood has replaced
the 'substance' of bread and wine, and that is what Aquinas
called 'transubstantiation'. But we should also pay attention to
the sense in which Aquinas says transubstantiation is not
'replacement'. Christ's flesh and blood has not 'taken the place'
of the bread and wine, if by that you mean the bread and wine
have been transformed into Christ's flesh and blood. That
Aquinas denies. Nor have Christ's flesh and blood squeezed

themselves into the dimensions formerly occupied by the bread and wine, into that place on the altar. Those dimensions and that place are part of what Aquinas calls the 'appearances' of bread and wine. They are *signs* of the real presence of Christ's body, but have not become real properties of his body; he retains his own dimensions and place wherever he is living resurrected at the moment. What has been 'replaced' is the real significance in God's eyes of those signs. The physico-chemical and nutritive and biological virtues of bread and wine persist in those appearances in every respect – they are not illusions 'deceiving' the senses. What is there analyses as chemical bread and wine; and in a phrase which often escapes commentators' notice, the 'individual existence' of that piece of bread remains, but now as the 'existence' of everything else about it but its 'substance'!

I think that Aquinas, faced with a modern terminology in which substance means chemical substance, would have had no difficulty in saying that the chemical substance of bread indeed remains as one of the 'appearances' under which the substance of Jesus's body is present. Perhaps because of the previous century's controversy, Aquinas made heavy going of his discussion of transubstantiation as a miracle, and distorted his own theological treatment of the Eucharist. The theology essential is his view of the Eucharist as the kiss of a God present to the touch, as a moment of love and friendship in action, nourishing and building up the mystical, sacramental body of the Church community.

This mystical body is open to the whole human race; it is God's society for the recreation and reordering of the cosmos, fulfilling in itself every kind of society devoted to the good of mankind and of the world. Nowadays people frequently complain that the Church is meddling in politics, and it does, just as it has meddled in religion all these centuries. But theologically the Church is neither a *polis*, a worldly state or city, nor a religion. The Church is Jesus's movement of human renewal, renewing the way we relate to God and the way we relate to our fellow men. In that sense the Church falls short of itself whenever it attempts to put on a merely worldly face, be that the face of a political society laying down laws or that of a religious society pontificating on morality.

It is noteworthy that Aquinas's treatment of these mystical and sacramental matters is the closest he gets to an ecclesiology, to a theology of the Church as such, this despite an enormous growth in papal power in his time. His own family had divided loyalties, at least one of his brothers supporting the secular cause of Frederick, the king of Sicily and Holy Roman Emperor, and another being executed by Frederick as a supporter of the Pope. In his political works there is an often remarked ambiguity as to whether the Pope has a political role or not. His sympathies seem to have lain with a division of authority between the secular and religious spheres. In Aquinas's mind the Church's duty of care extends to the good of the whole universe, but with an absolute obligation to exercise that mandate as its founder did, with total respect for the autonomy of human nature, and a total love for every individual born into it.

9

EVERLASTING LIFE

[a] We must portray the union of God's Word with a human being neither as a melting of two natures into one, nor as joining something essential to something external and accidental (as a person is connected with his house or his clothes). The Word of God truly became a man, subsisting in a human body and soul that incarnation had made truly his own . . . Now nothing in all creation is more like this than soul's union to body . . . not to body as its matter (for that would make one nature of God and man, just as matter and form make up one specific nature), but to body as its tool or organ . . . For body is soul's conjoint tool, dedicated to the work of one owner like a hand, not external like an axe used in common by many people. Compare the ways God is united to human beings. Everyone is God's tool – *God himself works in us our willing fulfilment of his good will* – but a separate and external tool moved to works not proper to God alone but common to all rational nature (like understanding truth and loving good and doing justice). Only Christ's human nature has been adopted as a tool to carry out works proper to God alone (cleansing from sin, enlightening minds with grace, and leading us to a

perfect and everlasting life). So Christ's human nature belongs to God as his conjoint and proper tool, like a hand to a soul. For it is not unusual to find something in nature acting as a proper tool of something that is not its form: as the organ of speech our tongue is proper to our understanding, though (as Aristotle proved) the understanding itself doesn't actualize any part of the body, and an individual can have a conjoint tool that is not natural to the species – a sixth finger, for example. So we can say that human nature is united to God's Word as a sort of conjoint tool, not having the Word as its form and not belonging to his nature, but nevertheless belonging to his person.

Summa contra Gentiles 4.41

[b] For persons to issue within the one nature of God there must be activity, not outgoing but indwelling, and in intellectual natures there are only two such activities: understanding and willing. From both these activities something finally issues: understanding ends with the conceiving of a word in the understanding mind (for until some conception stabilizes in our mind we have not yet understood but are still thinking in order to understand), and willing ends with the issuing of a love from the lover's will (since love is a stabilization of will in the good being willed). Now in creatures neither a word nor a love are subsistent persons having the nature of what does the understanding and willing; since in creatures to understand and to will are not to exist, but a sort of extra to the creature's nature. But in God to exist and to understand and to will are all the same thing, so that his Word and Love are not extras to the divine nature but subsist within it . . .

Understanding and willing, however, are differently ordered in God and ourselves. Our understanding takes in what it knows from outside sources and our willing tends towards outside goals, so that in us things come in to soul when we understand and soul goes out to things when we will. But God's knowledge causes rather than comes from things, and his will, rather than tending to an end outside, orders everything outside to himself as end. So, although in both God's and our understanding and willing there is a kind of circle (willing returning to where understanding began), our circle begins and ends outside while his comes to a close in himself . . . Now once a circle is closed nothing further can be added, so no third activity issues within God's nature; all further issuing takes place outside that nature. In God then there are only three persons: one who does not issue from another and two who do issue, one as a Love and the other as a Word.

Quaestio Disputata de Potentia Dei 9.9c

Here are two passages of theology from 1265 when Aquinas was teaching in Orvieto and in Rome. They ask how we can formulate with rational coherence the Christian teaching on the Trinity: the existence of three persons in God and their relations to their single divine nature; and in the case of one of them – the Son of God – his relation to two natures, divine and human. The first passage comes from the *Summa contra Gentiles* in which Aquinas attempted to present Christian doctrines to Muslim and pagan non-believers in such a way that, even if reason could not prove them true, they would not appear patently false. The second passage is extracted from a course of disputed questions argued as a master in Rome, and asks what is special about the number three. Why not two or four persons in God? It was composed a year or so after the *Summa contra Gentiles* was completed.

In both passages Aquinas tries to articulate these doctrines as precisely as human language allowed. Early Church councils had started this process of articulation many centuries earlier, trying to bring order into a multitude of warring interpretations of what the Christian scriptures had said about God as Father, Son and Holy Spirit and how God the Son had become truly a human being while remaining truly a divine person. Aquinas carefully treads between opposing errors, and seeks to expound orthodox formulas in such a way as to show their coherence with the philosophical view of the world he shares with his Muslim and pagan readers. What results is so cautiously put together that one can be forgiven for overlooking the boldness of what it actually says.

In the first passage, concerning Christ's one person and two natures, Aquinas works towards a reformulation in terms of existence: if Christ has the nature of God and the nature of man, has he two existences, one as God and one as man? What if we modelled the union of two natures in one person by saying that divinity defined what Christ essentially was and humanity was some externally existing addition, like clothes? Then there would be two existences in Christ, one essential and one accidental. There are, for example, ways in which Socrates can exist in a weak sense, either temporarily (being clothed) or permanently (being white), but neither of these are existence in the strong sense – Socrates's essential existence as Socrates. A person can have more than one existence in the weak sense – Socrates being white is not Socrates being musical – but not more than one existence in the strong sense. So if the Son of God's human nature had supervened on him externally, in a way unrelated to his personal existence, Christ would have had two existences, one as God in the strong sense as God and the other as man in a weak sense. His divinity would have defined what he essentially was, but his humanity wouldn't. His human existence would not have been a personal existence. That is at odds with the life described in the Gospels.

We must rather, Aquinas thinks, compare the way soul and body, form and matter, unite to make one existent thing. That however might land us in an opposite error: form and matter do not exist separately, they are factors that together constitute one nature and so produce one existent thing in one nature. But Christ, so the scriptures teach, had two births – one eternal and one in time – and so two natures (the word 'nature' derives from the word 'to be born'). He was born twice, yet was one person with one existence. At this point Aquinas makes a sideways move. We will compare the union in Christ with that of soul and body, but distinguish it from the union of form and matter. For besides being related as form to matter, soul is also related to body as agent to conjoined tool. Aquinas adopts this model of conjoined tool: the hand or arm that is joined to us and by which we wield all separate tools. A separate tool and the agent that wields it are two separately existing things, but the tool is joined to the agent in one activity – an activity which belongs to the tool (being determined by the tool's special nature) and yet prolongs in a sense the activity of its agent. A conjoined tool not only shares activity in this way with its agent, but is also an actual part of the agent, sharing one existence with it.

Existence and activity both belong to people and things by nature, Aquinas says in another place, but in different ways. Existence refers to the very realization of a thing as a thing, or a person as a person; a thing can have only one existence, which it shares with conjoined tools but not with separate ones. Activity is an effect of a thing or person determined by some form or nature that it has; diverse activities do not prejudice someone's personal unity, and any one activity can be shared with a tool that serves that activity, be it separate or personal. Moreover, the way in which a conjoined tool shares activity with its agent is more intimate than the way a separate tool does. A separate tool is available for use by other agents, but a conjoined tool is that agent's alone, dedicated to the agent and to whatever activity is special to that agent.

Since having an arm or an eye is all part of being the one person Socrates, Aquinas argues, if Socrates (already in existence as a person) happened to acquire another arm or eye (being born blind/had a transplant) he would not thereby acquire a new existence. What he would acquire is a sort of relationship to these extra additions, so that he existed now with parts added to those he had before. The Son of God indeed takes up something new in taking up human nature but not something extra; he takes up human nature not as something supervening and secondary, but as something contributing to him as person and subject. So the human nature brings with it no new personal existence, but only a new relationship of the personal existence he already enjoys to his new human nature. His person exists now not only under a divine nature but also under a human one. The existence of the Son of God becomes the existence of a man, when the Son of God is born at Bethlehem. Moreover, the human nature becomes the intimate and dedicated tool of a special activity of God, an activity that only he can do. It becomes the special tool of the forgiveness of sin and the saving of humanity.

Aquinas identifies the existence of God the Son with the existence of Christ. The existence of God does then, in a sense, animate the existence of Christ, as a soul does a body.

It is as if the Son of God, who in the world of his nature, ability and power, exists outside and beyond Christ, in the world of actuality and historical fact does not. Indeed, since God is his own existence, and the existence of Christ and God the Son are one, the very existence of Christ *is* God.

Such arguments can appear very barren. Their usefulness is to make non-believers, who think these doctrines absurd and easy to pillory, think again. But theology must not only be clever, it must lead to understanding. Theology should eventually be judged by whether it helps illuminate and endear to Aquinas's readers the human being and divine person, Jesus of Nazareth, that he is talking about. In some ways the barrenness is because an appreciation of Jesus that grew 'bottom up' in his lifetime is being formulated 'top down'. It grew from experience of him as a human being, and the consequent attempts to see that experience as a new revelation of God's person are being formulated by fitting together already constituted ideas of divine being and human being. We are employing a sort of logic or grammar of such ideas, and taking a step further will show what disappears behind the grammar.

Where does this divine personal life fit into the human being? we might ask. What must it disturb in that human being in order to make room for itself? How could a human being with such a presence within him preserve his finite human balance? Such questions all betray an idea of divine nature as needing room for one reason or another, perhaps because being divine is so huge and majestic that it really needs courts of angels around it to display its magnificence or power. But all the room God needs is there in a human being, because as part of their natural development, all human beings face the task of accepting being human, consenting to their creation. Dogs and crocodiles are not faced with this task: the humorist G.K. Chesterton once said that nobody claps a crocodile on the back and says 'Come on! Be a crocodile!' God's majesty is displayed in the New Testament not as surrounded by angels, but as a human being alone in agony in the Garden of Gethsemane the night before his crucifixion. God's majesty is displayed in willingly being human, at the mercy of the world he had created. And that fits without disturbance or distortion into the human nature we all possess. God's majesty lies in his divine consent to become a creature, a consent which finds its needed room in the human consent to live and die the life and death dealt out to one. The two consents are wedded, and the human willingness becomes, as Aquinas says, a sort of 'tongue' for the divine willingness. The more one reads Aquinas the more one uncovers this sort of idea dwelling inside the formulations; but sometimes our attention gets distracted from the idea by the details of its clever formulation.

The second extract is about the Trinity, the threefoldness of persons in one God, and shows a similar cleverness, arguing that the persons of God *can* be three but cannot be more than three, because threeness closes a certain circle and leaves nowhere else to go. The argument is so clear in the extract itself that its logic requires little comment, but again, if cleverness was all there was to the argument, we would find it very barren. The circle, however, is only a sort of epiphenomenon of the argument; the extract is really a meditation on the very centre of what Aquinas thinks life is, and on how every level of life is structured. It is, I would maintain, an image that underlies everything Aquinas had to say throughout his philosophy and theology, in the way Bergson believed a little whirlwind of an image underlay every great philosopher's thought.

For Aquinas sees the existence of everything as a stability

discovered in the flux of the ongoing world process. That stability has won the temporary favour of the environment it inhabits, an environment which itself has to have a certain stability within a larger environment. To exist is eventually to have the temporary favour of the whole universe as environment, the emergence of a 'self' within the favour of the universe. But this taking in from the universe is balanced by a giving out. The self contributes itself to the environment of other selves; it helps shape the flux into temporary order.

In D.H. Lawrence's poem 'The ballad of a man who has come through' he talks of 'the wind that blows through me', to which he would yield himself as a 'winged gift', a bird riding that wind; and in succeeding lines he changes that image to one of a willing chisel wielded by invisible hammer blows. Each self is a winged gift of the wind of this universe, something selved out of the flux and then returned to it as a gift. Aquinas is using the same image to explain the Christian doctrine of the Trinity: the coming out of the Son conceived from the unfathomable depths of the Father, and the return of the Son to the Father in the breathing forth of a Holy Spirit, a holy wind. He compares it to the way we conceive the world around us, and are then drawn to that world. Our origin and destination are the universe God created; God's origin and destination, so to speak, is the universal Father. And in Jesus Christ and the human race of which he is head (so runs the heart of Aquinas's reading of the Christian faith) these two join together. The whole of humanity and indeed the whole of the universe become the chisel of the invisible hammer blows of God.

CHRONOLOGY

About **1225** At the castle of Roccasecca, on the border between Papal territory to the north and the emperor Frederick's kingdom of Sicily to the south, halfway between Rome and Naples, Thomas was born to Theodora, wife to Landulf, a knight of the Aquino family. There were four sons (Thomas was the youngest) and five daughters.

1231–9 Aged 5–15, early schooling as an oblate monk at the Benedictine Abbey of Monte Cassino, ten miles to the south of Roccasecca, during a period of relative calm in hostilities between pope and emperor.

1239–44 Aged 15–20, early university studies at Naples, 80 miles south of Roccasecca, a secular university founded by Frederick in 1224 for the education of his governing officials.

1244 Aged 20, against his family's wishes joined the Dominicans (the Order of Preachers), founded in 1215. He fled north but was apprehended by his brother at Orvieto, 150 miles north of Roccasecca, to which he was returned for a year or so of imprisonment.

1245–8 On his release, the Dominicans sent him for his early training as a friar to Paris, under the aegis of a famous Dominican scholar, Albert the Great, originally from Germany.

1248–52 His first Dominican position as student assistant to Albert, who had founded a house of studies in Cologne.

1252–6 Sent, on Albert's recommendation, to teach theology at the university of Paris, as a 'bachelor' or graduate student. While there he lectured on scripture (the Old Testament books of *Isaiah* and *Jeremiah*), and on the accepted theological textbook of the day: Peter Lombard's *Sententiae* (Opinions).

1256–9 First period as master (professor) at Paris. The incumbent masters, all secular clergy, opposed the idea of masters from the new mendicant orders like the Franciscans and Dominicans, and one of Aquinas's works from this time is a defence of the mendicant orders entitled *Contra impugnantes*. His university course of disputed questions from this period are collected in his *Quaestiones disputatae de veritate,* and in *Quodlibets* 7–11. In addition Aquinas wrote a short commentary on the *De Trinitate* of Boethius (a fifth century Christian writer), and started his first *Summa* – the *Summa contra Gentiles.*

1259–61 Returned to Italy, whereabouts unknown (perhaps Naples), where he continued to work on volume 1 of his *Summa contra Gentiles.*

1261–5 Appointed lecturer to Dominican students at their friary in Orvieto. Completed the four-volume *Summa contra Gentiles,* and commented on the Old Testament book of *Job* and the new testament *Epistles of St Paul*. At the Pope's request, researched the differences between theologians of the Latin and Greek traditions (*Contra Errores Graecorum*), and started a collection of extracts from commentaries on the gospels by those theologians (*Catena Aurea* on Matthew).

1265–8 Appointed master at the general house of studies for Dominican students in Rome. For these students he began his greatest work, the *Summa Theologiae*, which would eventually replace Peter Lombard's *Sententiae* as the accepted theological textbook of the day. His courses of disputed questions from this time are collected as the *De Potentia*, the *De Anima* and the *De Spiritualibus Creaturis*. During this period he also completed his *Catena aurea* on Mark, Luke and John, and wrote a commentary on the *De Divinis Nominibus*, a theological work of great authority, since it was attributed at the time to St Dionysius (the patron saint of Paris and a disciple of St Paul). It is now known to be the work of a sixth century Syrian monk. Perhaps his *Compendium Theologiae*, a shorter work written for his secretary and unfinished, also dates from this time.

1268–72 Second period as master at the university of Paris. He worked throughout the period on the second volume of his *Summa Theologiae*. His course of disputed questions are collected as the *De Malo*, the *De Virtutibus* and the *De Unione Verbi Incarnati*, and as *Quodlibets* 1–6 and 12, and his scripture courses commented the gospels of Matthew and John and the epistles of Saint Paul. At this time the arts faculty of Paris was dominated by the followers of the Muslim commentator on Aristotle, Ibn Roschd (Averroes). Aquinas wrote short works distancing himself from Averroistic interpretations: *De aeternitate mundi* and *De unitate intellectus*, and he began a gigantic series of commentaries on Aristotle. He completed commentaries on Aristotle's *Physics* and *Ethics*, and started ones on the *De Interpretatione*, Book 2 of the *Posterior Analytics*, and the *Politics*. He again engaged in controversy about the ideals of the religious life with the secular masters of the university, producing the *De Perfectione Vitae Spiritualis* and the *Contra Retrahentes.*

1272–3 Aquinas returned to teach at his own study-house in Naples. Here he commented on Aristotle's *Metaphysics* (completed), *De Caelo* (incomplete) and *De Generatione* (incomplete). He also commented on a work attributed to Aristotle called the *De Causis*, and was the first to identify it as an Arabic summary of a work by the neo-Platonist philosopher Proclus. Aquinas lectured on the *Psalms*, and continued his work on the third volume of the *Summa Theologiae.*

1273–4 On or about 6 December 1273, Aquinas suffered a stroke, or some sort of trauma that prevented him from further work. However, he was summoned by the Pope to attend the Council of Lyon due to start in 1274. On the way there he was injured by the bough of a tree, and his condition rapidly deteriorated. He died on 7 March 1274, at the age of 49, in the Cistercian house at Fossanova, about 25 miles west of his birthplace.

SUGGESTIONS FOR FURTHER READING

Two indispensable websites map the vast material available on Aquinas. The first at www.thomisticum.org contains all the works of Aquinas in the best Latin texts available, with much else besides, including the superb search facility called the 'index thomisticus'. Though largely in Latin, the site can be navigated in English. The second at www.bonin/thomasbibliography contains a bibliography to all English translations and studies.

To read more of Aquinas himself, either pick up a volume of selections in English translation or concentrate on the *Summa Theologiae*. I recommend as volumes of selections:

McDermott, T., *Thomas Aquinas: Selected Philosophical Writings* (The World's Classics, Oxford University Press, 1993). (Restricted to philosophical texts, in flowing translation, arranged according to subject matter, with a good index.)

McInerny, R., *Thomas Aquinas: Selected Writings* (Penguin Classics, Penguin Books, 1998). (Philosophical and theological, in a more stilted translation, arranged chronologically, and without any index.)

If concentrating on the *Summa Theologiae*, then I recommend starting with:

McDermott, T., (1989) *St Thomas Aquinas: Summa Theologiae, a concise translation* (Christian Classics, Ave Maria Press, Notre Dame, 1989). (A one-volume condensation, with marginal references to the sixty-volume English/Latin version when one wants to expand reading on a particular topic.) Whichever strategy is adopted, the best way is to read the English side by side with the Latin (downloaded from the 'Aquinas in Latin' site above). Advice to those with little or no Latin is available on the thomasbibliography site. Readers without Latin should not despair: Aquinas's Latin is very basic. Rather than attempt to learn Latin from a textbook, why not try to learn Aquinas's Latin from persevering with his text, with copies of the original and an English translation open before one, and on the side a medium-size Latin dictionary containing a summary of Latin grammar (the *Pocket Oxford Latin Dictionary* is one such)? At present on the <u>thomisticum</u> site above, under 'Links, Texts and Versions' (*nexus interretiales, textus et versiones*), there is a reference to <u>http://krystal.op.cz/sth/settings.php</u>, which allows one to display the complete Latin and English texts of the *Summa Theologiae* side by side on the computer screen.

Finally, some recommended secondary material:

Life

Chesterton, G.K., *Saint Thomas Aquinas* (Hodder and Stoughton, 1933). (Lively and percipient.)

Torrell, J-P., *Saint Thomas Aquinas, vol 1: The Person and his Work* (Catholic University of America, 1996). (The most up-to-date discussion.)

Weisheipl, J.A., *Friar Thomas d'Aquino. His Life, Thought and Works* (Catholic University of America, 1983). (The best previous discussion in English.)

Studies

Davies, B., *The Thought of Thomas Aquinas* (Clarendon Press, 1992). (Good solid introduction to both the philosophy and the theology.)

Kerr, F., *After Aquinas, Versions of Thomism* (Blackwell Publishing, 2002). (Incisive discussion of whether Aquinas can survive his interpreters, philosophical and theological.)

Kretzmann, N. & Stump, E. (eds.), *The Cambridge Companion to the Philosophy of Aquinas* (Cambridge University Press, 1993). (An uneven collection of essays arranged by subject matter, philosophy only.)

The first two works have good bibliographies to guide into even further reading.

INDEX